D0772639

The March from Selma to Montgomery

Lucent Library of Black History

Other titles in this series:

The March from Selma to Montgomery

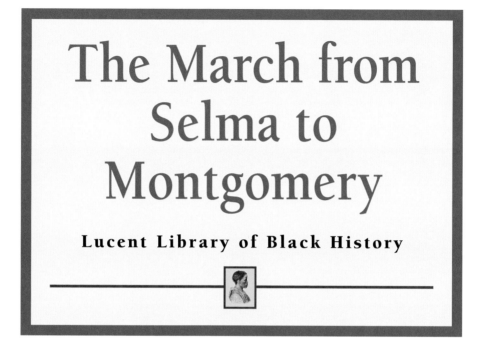

Lucent Library of Black History

Michael V. Uschan

LUCENT BOOKS
A part of Gale, Cengage Learning

GALE
CENGAGE Learning

Detroit • New York • San Francisco • New Haven, Conn • Waterville, Maine • London

LIBRARY OF CONGRESS CATALOGING-IN-PUBLICATION DATA

Uschan, Michael V., 1948-
  The march from Selma to Montgomery / by Michael V. Uschan.
    p. cm. -- (Lucent library of Black history)
  Includes bibliographical references and index.
  ISBN 978-1-4205-0571-9 (hardcover)
  1. Selma to Montgomery Rights March (1965 : Selma, Ala.) 2. African Americans--Civil rights--Alabama--Selma--History--20th century. 3. African Americans--Suffrage--Alabama--Selma--History--20th century. 4. Civil rights movements--Alabama--Selma--History--20th century. 5. Selma (Ala.)--Race relations--History--20th century. I. Title.
  F334.S4U73 2011
  324.6'2'08996073--dc22
                                                              2010050810

Lucent Books
27500 Drake Rd.
Farmington Hills, MI 48331

ISBN-13: 978-1-4205-0571-9
ISBN-10: 1-4205-0571-8

Printed in the United States of America
1 2 3 4 5 6 7 15 14 13 12 11

Printed by Bang Printing, Brainerd, MN, 1 Ptg., 06/2011

Contents

Foreword

It has been more than 500 years since Africans were first brought to the New World in shackles, and over 140 years since slavery was formally abolished in the United States. Over 50 years have passed since the fallacy of "separate but equal" was obliterated in the American courts, and some 40 years since the watershed Civil Rights Act of 1964 guaranteed the rights and liberties of all Americans, especially those of color. Over time, these changes have become celebrated landmarks in American history. In the twenty-first century, African American men and women are politicians, judges, diplomats, professors, deans, doctors, artists, athletes, business owners, and home owners. For many, the scars of the past have melted away in the opportunities that have been found in contemporary society. Observers such as Peter N. Kirsanow, who sits on the U.S. Commission of Civil Rights, point to these accomplishments and conclude, "The growing black middle class may be viewed as proof that most of the civil rights battles have been won."

In spite of these legal victories, however, prejudice and inequality have persisted in American society. In 2003, African Americans comprised just 12 percent of the nation's population, yet accounted for 44 percent of its prison inmates and 24 percent of its poor. Racially motivated hate crimes continue to appear on the pages of major newspapers in many American cities. Furthermore, many African Americans still experience either overt or muted racism in their daily lives. A 1996 study undertaken by Professor Nancy Krieger of the Harvard School of Public Health, for example, found that 80 percent of the African American participants reported having experienced racial discrimination in one or more settings, including at work or school, applying for housing and medical care, from the police or in the courts, and on the street or in a public setting.

It is for these reasons that many believe the struggle for racial equality and justice is far from over. These episodes of discrimination threaten to shatter the illusion that America has completely overcome its racist past, causing many black Americans to become increasingly frustrated and confused. Scholar and writer Ellis Cose has described this splintered state in the following way: "I have done everything I was supposed to do. I have stayed out of trouble with the law, gone to the right schools, and worked myself nearly to death. What more do they want? Why in God's name won't they accept me as a full human being?" For Cose and others, the struggle for equality and justice has yet to be fully achieved.

In many subtle yet important ways the traumatic experiences of slavery and segregation continue to inform the way race is discussed and experienced in the twenty-first century. Indeed, it is possible that America will always grapple with the fallout from its distressing past. Ulric Haynes, dean of the Hofstra University School of Business has said, "Perhaps race will always matter, given the historical circumstances under which we came to this country." But studying this past and understanding how it contributes to present-day dialogues about race and history in America is a critical component of contemporary education. To this end, the Lucent Library of Black History offers a thorough look at the experiences that have shaped the black community and the American people as a whole. Annotated bibliographies provide readers with ideas for further research, while fully documented primary and secondary source quotations enhance the text. Each book in the series explores a different episode of black history; together they provide students with a wealth of information as well as launching points for further study and discussion.

The Importance of the March

In March 1965 three hundred African Americans walked 54 miles (86.9km) from Selma, Alabama, to Montgomery, the state's capital, to demand that the government protect their voting rights. The Selma to Montgomery march was the historic culmination of the centuries-long battle African Americans waged for their civil rights. Forty-five years later in March 2010, the forty-fifth anniversary celebration of the historic protest included a reenactment of the march. Samuel F. Mosteller, state president of the Georgia chapter of the Southern Christian Leadership Conference (SCLC), was one of two dozen people who duplicated the march. The anniversary marchers set out from Selma on March 8 and ended their journey with a joyous rally at the capital on March 13. Mosteller told several hundred people in Montgomery why the reenactment was important: "Jews haven't forgotten the Holocaust and [neither] will we. Black folks need to remember their history."[1]

The Holocaust was the Nazi genocide of 6 million Jews during World War II. Jewish people throughout the world keep alive memories of that terrible time so that something like that will never happen again. Mosteller wants African Americans to remember their own painful history—the way millions of them were mistreated and violently oppressed in the United States for more than three centuries until they gained full political power with passage of the 1965 Voting Rights Act. The historic march is important because it was pivotal in convincing Congress to pass the measure that finally gave blacks the political power they needed to try to gain equality with whites.

A Right Long Denied

The first Africans arrived in 1619 in the English colony of Virginia. Until the end of the Civil War in 1865, millions of African Americans lived in slavery—first in thirteen English colonies and, starting in 1776, in the nation those colonies formed that became the United States of America. But even after slavery ended, racist whites for another century continued to deny blacks many basic rights the U.S. Constitution guaranteed every citizen. The most powerful right withheld from blacks was the right to vote. Without the power to elect officials who would protect their other rights, blacks were left at the mercy of whites, who dominated blacks by passing racist laws that restricted where they could work, live, eat, shop, and go to school.

In the first half of the twentieth century, conditions improved for African Americans in most of the nation because more of them began voting to elect officials who would protect their rights. But as late as the early 1960s, blacks in southern states remained politically powerless because state and local officials enforced racist laws making it difficult for African Americans to vote. Southern whites fought ferociously to deny blacks this right because they knew that the large population of blacks in southern states would then have the political power to achieve equality with whites.

The Reverend Martin Luther King Jr. was the most powerful leader of a new civil rights drive begun in the 1950s that had succeeded in toppling many racist laws that segregated blacks from whites. He had known from the beginning of the civil rights crusade that the right to vote was key to blacks' achieving equality. During a rally in Washington, D.C., on May 17, 1957, King gave his famous "Give Us the Ballot" speech to fifteen thousand people gathered on the steps of the Lincoln Memorial. King told them: "The denial of this sacred right is a tragic betrayal of the highest mandates of our democratic tradition. And so our most urgent request to the president of the United States and every member of Congress is to give us the right to vote. Give us the ballot, and we will no longer have to worry the federal government about our basic rights."[2]

On January 2, 1965, King brought the battle for that right to Selma, the seat of Dallas County in Alabama, where only three hundred of the county's fifteen thousand voting-age blacks were registered to vote. In a speech to several hundred people at Brown Chapel African Methodist Episcopal Church, King promised to help blacks exercise their right to vote. King would succeed in his goal but only after a series of bloody, dramatic events that showcased the plight of blacks to the entire world.

Wielding billy clubs and firing tear gas, Alabama state troopers and Dallas County sheriff's deputies confront peaceful civil rights marchers at the Pettus Bridge on March 7, 1965.

Three Marches

In the next three months King, Selma blacks, and white and black supporters from around the nation waged a fierce fight to secure the right to vote. First came weeks of protests in January and February in which thousands of men, women, and children were arrested and beaten. In a dramatic finale to the drive, hundreds of African Americans on March 7 began a 51-mile walk (82km) from Selma to Montgomery. When marchers crossed the Pettus Bridge leading out of town, they were met by Alabama state troopers, Dallas County sheriff's deputies, and angry civilians. Wielding billy clubs and bullwhips and firing tear gas, the whites, some of them riding horses, violently attacked the peaceful marchers on what became known as Bloody Sunday. Seventy demonstrators were injured in the ensuing carnage, seventeen of them severely enough to be hospitalized. The scenes of brutality against the marchers shocked the world when they were shown on television.

Bloody Sunday was the first of three attempts to march to Montgomery. Two days after Bloody Sunday, King led about twenty-five hundred black and white marchers back to the Pettus Bridge. After a prayer session, King walked marchers back into Selma to obey a court order that barred further marches until a federal court hearing on the legality of the march could be held. The symbolic march was held to generate publicity about voting rights and show racist law enforcement officials that blacks would not abandon their goal of marching to Montgomery.

When the federal government overturned the court order barring the protest, eight thousand people gathered on March 21 at Brown Chapel for the start of the march to Montgomery. For the next four days, black and white supporters of black voting rights walked from Selma to Alabama's state capital. On the final day, fifty thousand people gathered in Montgomery to celebrate the successful march.

The march and protests during the three-month voting rights campaign had far-reaching consequences. Violence against blacks demanding a right the Constitution guaranteed them angered President Lyndon Baines Johnson so much that on March 15 he introduced a Voting Rights Act to Congress. Less than four months later

Johnson signed the historic bill, which had enforcement procedures that finally gave southern blacks the most important right citizens can have.

The Result of Bloody Sunday

John Lewis was one of the leaders of the Selma to Montgomery March and a victim on Bloody Sunday when law enforcement officials beat him unconscious at the foot of the Pettus Bridge. When Lewis returned to Selma in 2010 to celebrate the march's forty-fifth anniversary, he said it had been worth getting beaten to gain that right because "what came to be known as Bloody Sunday changed America forever."[3] Lewis was part of that change. Once their voting rights were protected, blacks began electing federal, state, and local officials who supported their rights. Lewis himself was elected to Congress in 1987 and in the next two decades became one of that body's most highly respected members.

Chapter One

The Modern Civil Rights Movement

On the afternoon of December 1, 1955, Rosa Parks boarded a bus in downtown Montgomery, Alabama, to head home after working as a seamstress at a department store. She sat in the rear of the bus because the front seats were reserved for whites. Riding in the back of the bus was one of many daily humiliations blacks in southern states had to endure because of racist laws regulating segregation of the races. When the bus Parks was on became crowded, driver James F. Blake ordered Parks and several other blacks to surrender their seats to white passengers. Parks refused. She remained seated even after Blake threatened to have her arrested for not obeying his order. Parks explained years later that she made a spontaneous decision to fight the injustice of segregation: "Just having paid for a seat and riding for only a couple of blocks and then having to stand was too much. There had to be a stopping place [for submitting to racist treatment], and this seemed to have been the place for me to stop being pushed around and to find out what human rights I had, if any."[4]

Parks's act of defiance is considered the beginning of the decade-long civil rights battle that culminated with the Selma to Montgomery march and helped African Americans achieve equality under the law with whites. But historian Fred Powledge

Rosa Parks, pictured on the aisle in dark coat and hat, rides a bus. Some date the beginning of the civil rights movement from Parks's refusal to give up her seat to a white passenger on a Montgomery bus.

believes the civil rights movement was the result of more than one lone act of courage. He has written that "the civil rights movement was not something spontaneous, but the inevitable outcome of centuries of mistreatment of black people by white people and their governments."[5] That racially motivated abuse began when the first blacks came to the land that would one day become the United States of America.

Slavery and Segregation

When the first twenty Africans arrived in the English colony of Virginia in 1619, they arrived in chains and were sold as laborers. For the next two centuries, millions of African Americans lived and died as slaves. Slavery continued even after the United States was founded in 1783 on the political ideal set forth in the Declaration of Independence in 1776 that "all men are created equal."

Northern states abolished slavery in the late eighteenth century, but Southern states continued it as a source of cheap labor for their agriculture-based economies. Tension over slavery between Northern and Southern states mounted in the nineteenth century. That tension exploded into the Civil War in 1861 because Southern states were sure President Abraham Lincoln would abolish slavery. The North won the conflict in 1865 and freed all slaves. To ensure African Americans would remain free and have the rights of other citizens, the nation approved three amendments to the U.S. Constitution. The Thirteenth Amendment in 1865 abolished slavery, the Fourteenth Amendment in 1868 granted citizenship to African Americans, and the Fifteenth Amendment in 1870 declared no one could deny citizens their rights because of race.

How Whites Denied Blacks the Vote

For nearly a century after the end of Reconstruction, southern states used a variety of ways to keep African Americans from voting. One was the poll tax, a fee to vote that many poor blacks could not afford to pay. Another was the literacy test, which was not an examination of reading ability but a test of knowledge of the state's constitution that included questions on obscure state laws. Local registrars also used several tricks to stop blacks from registering. If a black person came to register, officials closed the office or simply refused to register them. On election day, voting officials put the polling places in white areas that black voters might fear to enter, or they moved the polling places without posting notices where blacks could find out about the changes. In addition to threats of violence, white citizens also used economic coercion to stop black voting. Historian Fred Powledge explains: "Economic pressure was a major technique used to keep blacks from voting. A Negro farmer who tried to register could have his credit cut off and find it impossible to buy fuel for his tractor; a black schoolteacher could lose her job. And blacks who were not directly affected by such actions could see from them that perhaps it was best not to register."

Fred Powledge. *Free at Last? The Civil Rights Movement and the People Who Made It*. Boston: Little, Brown, 1991, p. 131.

The amendments, however, failed to secure those rights for long for southern blacks. In the final decades of the nineteenth century, southern states passed laws that segregated the races and denied blacks those rights. Southerners called this segregation Jim Crow. It was the stage name of a nineteenth-century white entertainer who had mocked African Americans by painting his face dark and singing songs and telling jokes that ridiculed blacks. Jim Crow laws were enforced by state and local governments. They made blacks second-class citizens by barring them from eating at restaurants, staying at hotels, shopping at stores, attending schools, or using bathrooms reserved for whites. Jim Crow even followed blacks after death because cemeteries were also segregated.

Jim Crow still existed in the 1950s because eleven southern states—Alabama, Arkansas, Florida, Georgia, Louisiana, Mississippi, North Carolina, South Carolina, Tennessee, Texas, and Virginia—were able to deny blacks the right to vote by enacting legal barriers that made it almost impossible for blacks to vote. Racist whites acting as individuals also used violence to keep blacks from voting. Whites did this because they knew that if the multitude of blacks who lived in the South could vote, they would elect officials who would end segregation and discrimination. But in the second half of the twentieth century, southern blacks developed a new determination to fight for their rights. And in a few short years they ended Jim Crow and won legal equality with whites.

A New Attitude

This new, more militant attitude started after World War II when black soldiers and sailors resented being denied their rights after they returned home from fighting for their country. James Hicks saw combat in the Pacific against Japan. He explains the feeling those warriors had: "I think that when black veterans of World War II returned home, they were really an influence on their communities. [They] felt, 'I paid my dues over there and I'm not going to take this anymore over here.'"[6]

African Americans were also emboldened to fight for their rights when the federal government finally began enforcing equal rights. The National Association for the Advancement of Colored People (NAACP), in February 1951, filed a federal class-action lawsuit against the Topeka, Kansas, Board of Education. The case was

These African American students and their parents sued the Topeka Board of Education over the segregation of the city's schools. On May 17, 1954, the U.S. Supreme Court unanimously found that separate but equal schools violated the rights of black students.

called *Brown v. Board of Education.* The suit claimed the city's segregated school system denied black children the same quality of education students received at white schools. On May 17, 1954, the U.S. Supreme Court ruled 9-0 that separate but equal schools violated the rights of black students. The decision says: "In the field of public education, the doctrine of separate but equal has no place. Separate educational facilities are inherently unequal. [Thus black students are] deprived of the equal protection of the laws guaranteed by the Fourteenth Amendment."[7]

The Fourteenth Amendment prohibits states from denying citizens their constitutional rights, but the federal government had long ignored states that discriminated against blacks. In fact,

When Blacks Could Vote

Although southern blacks had to fight for their civil rights in the 1950s and 1960s, for a brief time in U.S. history they freely exercised all of their rights, including the right to vote. This was during Reconstruction, the period from the end of the Civil War in 1865 until 1877, when the federal government oversaw the restructuring of local and state governments in Southern states. African Americans were able to enjoy those rights because U.S. soldiers occupying Southern states protected them against racist whites who wanted to continue to treat them as second-class citizens. During Reconstruction, blacks not only voted in large numbers but were elected to public office at all levels from county sheriff to the U.S. Senate. In Louisiana in 1872, African American Pinckney Benton Stewart Pinchback even served briefly as governor. There were so many black state legislators and officials that historian Eric Foner claims Reconstruction in the South created the first multiracial system of government in the world. When Reconstruction ended and U.S. soldiers were withdrawn from Southern states, whites regained control of government and began taking rights away from blacks. And because whites denied blacks the right to vote, they were politically powerless to gain them back for nearly a century.

the high court in 1896 had provided legal justification for discriminatory Jim Crow laws in *Plessy v. Ferguson*. Homer Plessy of Louisiana had claimed his Fourteenth Amendment rights were violated when he was denied a seat in a white railroad car. The court threw out his lawsuit and claimed that "[if] one race be inferior to the other socially, the Constitution of the United States cannot put them on the same plane."[8]

The ruling allowed states to provide separate facilities for blacks and whites if they were equal in quality. Even though black facilities in southern states, from restrooms to schools, were always inferior, southern states used the ruling to justify segregation. The *Brown* ruling gave blacks new hope the federal government would protect their rights. That hope, like Parks's bravery, helped ignite the civil rights movement.

Victory in Montgomery

On December 5, 1955, Parks was convicted of violating a 1945 Alabama bus segregation law and fined fourteen dollars. When influential Montgomery blacks met later that day, they decided to protest the law by having blacks boycott the bus system. They also decided to file a lawsuit claiming the segregation was unconstitutional. What surprised the black community was their choice of a protest leader—the Reverend Martin Luther King Jr. King, pastor of Dexter Avenue Baptist Church, was just twenty-six and had lived in Montgomery for only a few months. Many

The Reverend Martin Luther King Jr. delivers a sermon at the Dexter Avenue Baptist Church. The unknown King gave a powerful, emotional speech in Montgomery, and many in the black community immediately embraced him as their leader.

of the five thousand people at a protest rally that evening did not even know King. But in a powerful, inspirational speech, King won their hearts and began his historic fight for civil rights. King eloquently explained why blacks were ready to fight segregation: "We are here to say to those who have mistreated us so long that we are tired [of] being kicked about by the brutal feet of oppression."[9] Then, in a step that would shape the coming civil rights movement, King declared that the protest had to be nonviolent:

> Now, let us say that we are not here advocating violence, we have overcome that. I want it to be known throughout Montgomery and throughout this nation that we are *Christian* people. . . . But the great glory of American democracy is the right to protest for right. . . . If we are wrong, then the Supreme Court of this nation is wrong. . . . If we are wrong, God Almighty is wrong.[10]

Montgomery's fifty thousand blacks composed less than half of the population of Alabama's capital but three-fourths of its bus system's riders. By refusing to ride the bus, Montgomery blacks dealt an economic as well as a moral blow against segregation. Because so many poor blacks did not have cars, the protest group mobilized a car pool to drive people where they needed to go.

King's charismatic leadership and the violent response by whites to the protest generated national media coverage of the boycott. In addition to attacking blacks waiting for free rides, racist whites bombed the homes of several protest leaders. When King's home was struck on January 30, 1956—the bomb damaged the family's front porch, but his family was not injured—angry blacks who gathered at his home demanded vengeance against the bombers. King calmed them by saying "We must love our white brothers no matter what they do to us. [Jesus] still cries out across the centuries: 'Love your enemies.' We must learn to meet hate with love."[11] King's decision to stick to his pledge of nonviolence even after his family had been endangered impressed people around the world.

The U.S. Supreme Court ruled on November 13, 1956, that laws segregating bus seating were unconstitutional. The court decision that overturned the bus law was the first major victory African Americans won through protest. The pattern of the

Montgomery boycott—protesters using nonviolence against racist whites who usually fought back with billy clubs, bombs, and bullets—became the standard for civil rights protests in the following decade that slowly began to give southern blacks rights that had long been denied them.

Fighting Jim Crow

On February 1, 1960, four freshmen at North Carolina Agricultural and Technical College in Greensboro followed in King's peaceful footsteps to protest segregation at a Woolworth's Five & Dime Store. After buying school supplies, something blacks were allowed to do, Ezell Blair Jr., David Richmond, Joseph McNeil, and Franklin McCain sat down at 4 P.M. at the all-white lunch counter and ordered cups of coffee. When a waitress told them, "We don't serve coloreds here,"[12] they remained seated until the store closed ninety minutes later. They returned the next day to

College students (from left to right) Joseph Mitchell, Franklin McCain, Billy Smith, and Clarence Henderson started a sit-in at the whites-only counter at the Woolworth's in Greensboro, North Carolina, on February, 1, 1960. The sit-in movement quickly spread to cities throughout the South.

continue the protest with sixteen more students; they inspired a series of similar protests, called sit-ins, throughout the South.

Sit-in protests had failed in the past because they were sporadic and short-lived. But in the next twelve months more than seventy thousand people, most of them high school and college students, staged sit-ins in more than a hundred southern cities. Supporters, both black and white, also began economic boycotts of racist businesses. In addition to trying to integrate restaurants, protesters attempted to check out books at public libraries, shop at stores, and watch movies at theaters reserved for whites.

Southern white officials and citizens fought back to preserve segregation. Police arrested more than thirty-six hundred protesters, often on made-up or bogus charges, and racist individuals beat protesters. An example of white violence occurred on April 14, 1961, in Biloxi, Mississippi. When blacks staged a "wade-in" at a white beach on the Gulf of Mexico, people armed with iron pipes, chains, and baseball bats attacked them. Police ignored the brutality. One officer even told Gilbert Mason, who had organized the protest, to get off the beach or he would shoot him. Fisk University student Diane Nash led sit-ins in Nashville, Tennessee. She explains how terrifying it was to protest while angry whites cursed and threatened her: "[Although people told me] how brave I was for sitting in and marching I was wall-to-wall terrified. I can remember sitting in class many times [when] I knew we were going to have a demonstration that afternoon. I was really afraid."[13]

John Lewis was another Fisk University student and protest leader. On April 17, 1960, Lewis helped organize the Student Nonviolent Coordinating Committee (SNCC), which began coordinating protests throughout the South. Less than a month later, on May 10, Lewis wrote about a victory in Nashville: "Six downtown stores we had marched on, sat in and been arrested at during the previous three months served food to black customers for the first time in the city's history."[14] Lewis said the protests succeeded because boycotts hurt businesses so much financially that their owners were forced to integrate.

When businesses in other cities soon began integrating, blacks became bold enough to challenge other forms of Jim Crow.

Protests and Violence

In the spring of 1961, black and white protesters began a series of Freedom Rides to integrate interstate travel. Blacks traveling between states were still forced to sit in certain sections on the bus, and bus stations had segregated facilities. On May 4, 1961, seven blacks and six whites split into two groups to board Greyhound and Trailways buses in Washington, D.C. Their protest trips to New Orleans would carry them though states like Alabama, where whites were desperately trying to preserve segregation.

The first violence occurred at the Greyhound station in Rock Hill, South Carolina, when whites beat up Lewis and Albert Bigelow, who was white, for entering the white waiting room. At the stop in Anniston, Alabama, members of the Ku Klux Klan (KKK) armed with pistols, clubs, chains, and knives surrounded the bus. Riders stayed on the bus for their own safety, but someone slashed the bus's tires before it left the station. The tires went flat six miles out of the city, and after the vehicle stopped, someone threw a firebomb through a bus window. When passengers got off the burning bus, whites beat them. The Trailways bus was also attacked in Anniston when racist whites forced their way onto the vehicle, beat riders, and forced blacks to the rear of the bus.

A Greyhound bus used by Freedom Riders sits burning outside Anniston, Alabama, in May 1961. Racist whites slashed the tires of the bus and threw a firebomb in a window.

The Greyhound bus could not continue the trip, but the Trailways bus drove on to Birmingham. When it arrived on May 14, twenty whites armed with metal pipes beat passengers as they got off the bus. So many riders were injured that the trip was canceled. Nash had not been on the buses but the Student Nonviolent Coordinating Committee (SNCC) leader believed the ride should continue. Nash called the Reverend Fred L. Shuttlesworth, an SCLC leader, and promised she would find volunteers to continue the ride. When Shuttlesworth told her, "Young lady, do you know that the Freedom Riders were almost killed here?" she responded, "Yes, and this is exactly why the Ride must not be stopped."[15] On May 20 two dozen students recruited by Nash left Birmingham for Montgomery, where whites again attacked them.

The Freedom Rides continued for weeks despite the danger and the fact that hundreds of riders were arrested. Media coverage of the protest forced then-president John F. Kennedy to act. On May 29, 1961, Kennedy ordered the U.S. Justice Department to issue a regulation banning segregation in interstate terminals. It went into effect on November 1.

Victories such as those that southern blacks were achieving were piecemeal, and they had to keep fighting almost community by community to win them. Blacks gradually realized that to achieve equality, voting was the right they needed most. Lawrence Guyot, a SNCC leader, explains the importance of voting: "If you sit at a lunch counter, you're either served or you're not served, and that's it. But once you get [the right to vote], everything else happens. Everything else flows from that [because it results in political power]."[16]

SNCC and other groups soon began campaigns to help southern blacks vote.

Registering Voters

In June 1960 when the Reverend June Dowdy tried to register to vote in Fayette County, Mississippi, he had trouble finding the correct office. Dowdy said when he asked a white man where to register, "[he] directed me to go down to Hatchie Bottom. That's the swamp along the Hatchie River where a Negro was lynched back about 1940 after he tried to vote."[17] The threat of violence against African Americans who wanted to vote was one of many reasons only seventeen blacks had cast votes in Fayette County from 1952 through 1959 even though they made up nearly 70

King Seeks the Right to Vote

On May 17, 1957, the Reverend Martin Luther King Jr. spoke to fifteen thousand people in Washington, D.C., during a civil rights rally. He told them why blacks needed to be able to vote:

> The denial of this sacred right is a tragic betrayal of the highest mandates of our democratic tradition. [Give] us the ballot, and we will no longer have to worry the federal government about our basic rights. Give us the ballot, and we will no longer plead to the federal government for passage of an anti-lynching law; we will by the power of our vote write the law on the statute books of the South and bring an end to the dastardly acts of the hooded perpetrators of violence. Give us the ballot, and we will transform the salient misdeeds of bloodthirsty mobs into the calculated good deeds of orderly citizens. Give us the ballot, and we will fill our legislative halls with men of goodwill and send to the sacred halls of Congress men who will [honor black rights]. Give us the ballot and we will place judges on the benches of the South who will do justly and love mercy, and we will place at the head of the southern states governors who will [help and not hurt blacks].

Martin Luther King Jr. "Give Us the Ballot," address delivered at the Prayer Pilgrimage for Freedom, May 17, 1957, Washington, D.C. www.stanford.edu/group/King/papers/vol4/570517.004-Give_Us_the_Ballot.html.

Martin Luther King Jr. delivers his "Give Us the Ballot" speech to civil rights protesters at the Prayer Pilgrimage for Freedom in Washington, D.C., on May 17, 1957.

percent of the county's population. That was better than neighboring Haywood County, where no African American had voted since Reconstruction had ended nearly a century earlier.

Mississippi was one of the most heavily segregated and racist southern states—in 1960 only 6 percent of voting-age blacks were registered, and in thirteen counties none were registered at all. In July 1961 Robert Moses, a teacher from New York, led SNCC's first voter registration drive. SNCC set up Freedom Schools in several Mississippi counties to teach blacks how to fill out complex registration applications and facts about their state constitution they needed to know for a literacy exam. Moses said it was hard to find people willing to register because they feared what would happen to them. "In Amite County," Moses said, "most of the people were afraid to go down to the courthouse to register."[18]

Those fears were soon realized. In August, when Moses tried to register voters in the town of Liberty in Amite County, he was beaten and suffered a head wound that required nine stitches. In a separate Amite County incident Herbert Lee, a black farmer, was shot to death by a state legislator who claimed Lee attacked him. Both the person who beat Moses and the man who shot Lee were charged, but white juries found both men innocent of any crimes in the attacks.

Racist violence and intimidation often came from law enforcement officials who were supposed to protect citizens. In July 1962 blacks held a voter registration meeting in Sasser, Georgia, at Mount Olive Baptist Church. Terrell County sheriff Z.T. Mathews and two deputies showed up at the church in an attempt to scare them into stopping the drive. The armed officers, tapping billy clubs in the palms of their hands, walked around making negative remarks about black voting. When a reporter asked Mathews why he was there, he responded, "We want our colored people to go on living like they have for the last hundred years."[19] That sentiment was one shared by many racist whites in the South.

The most brutal example of such racist law enforcement occurred during the 1964 Freedom Summer, a massive effort involving one thousand volunteers from around the nation who went to Mississippi to help blacks register to vote. In June, three voter registration workers—Andrew Goodman and Michael Schwerner, white volunteers from northern states, and Mississippi native James Earl Chaney, who was black—disappeared in Neshoba County while investigating the burning of a black church. On June 21 Neshoba County deputies arrested the workers for driving over the speed limit, but they were never seen again. Federal officials later proved the deputies had killed them and hidden their bodies. At the funeral for the slain civil rights workers, Fannie L. Chaney, James Earl's mother, said: "All Mississippi Negroes should now stand up for their rights. Since my son has been murdered, if we don't stand up for our civil rights now, his death will have been in vain, and the deaths of the other two boys."[20]

Southern blacks and their white supporters did continue fighting, and the battle soon took them to Alabama.

On to Selma

The drive to register southern black voters in the early 1960s helped create some new voters, but by the end of 1964, 3 million of the 5 million southern blacks of voting age were still not able to cast ballots. The percentages were especially low in rural areas like Dallas County, Alabama, where blacks composed 57 percent of the population. Because only 335 of 15,115 voting-age blacks were registered, they had no political power even though they outnumbered white voters. This injustice made Selma, the Dallas County seat, a perfect place to challenge racist policies that denied blacks the right to vote. And in 1965 it would draw King there to begin one of the most dramatic events of his storied fight for civil rights.

Chapter Two

Battle for the Ballot in Selma

In 1965 Amelia Boynton was one of the few African American voters in Selma, Alabama. Boynton registered to vote in 1930 and since then had tried to help other blacks become voters. That was difficult because Dallas County officials did everything possible to eliminate potential voters, including rejecting them for the slightest mistake in filling out registration forms. Boynton said that when an elderly man she was helping accidentally wrote off the line on his application, the registrar immediately told him his penmanship mistake disqualified him. The man responded angrily by saying: "Mr. White Man, you can't tell me that I can't register. I'll try anyway. For I own a hundred and forty acres of land [and] I took these hands that I have and made crops to put [ten children] through school. If I'm not worthy of being a registered voter, then God have mercy on this city."[21]

The registrar let the man complete the form but denied his application. Boynton said that was normal in Dallas County and that in one eight-year period fewer than twenty-five blacks succeeded in becoming registered voters there. Boynton in 1962 invited SNCC to Selma to end such indignities and injustice.

SNCC Arrives

When Bernard Lafayette first came through Selma in 1961 as a Freedom Rider, so many angry whites were at the bus station that his bus did not stop. The twenty-two-year-old Baptist minister did not receive a much warmer reception when he came to Selma, the Dallas County seat, to begin a statewide Alabama voter registration drive the following year. When Lafayette arrived in November 1962 to begin preparations for the drive, police officers and sheriff's deputies began following him to record his movements and intimidate him.

Although Boynton and members of the Dallas County Voters League (DCVL) were eager to help register voters, Lafayette discovered that many African Americans did not want to become involved. They told Lafayette, "We ain't got no business meddling in white folks' business,"[22] which meant they were afraid to help him because whites would punish them for trying to vote. "The fear," Lafayette said, "was very thick."[23]

Selma was a stronghold of segregation and racism. In the nineteenth century Selma had been a major cotton-producing center and slave market and, during the Civil War, a key supply depot for the Confederate army. Its reputation for being tough on blacks was maintained in the 1960s by racist, violent whites and county sheriff Jim Clark, a relentless foe of racial equality. He wore a badge that said NEVER, which referred to desegregation, and once told his wife he would "not let the n****** take over the whole state of Alabama."[24] When Selma blacks petitioned the city to desegregate schools, whites beat some people who signed the petition and threatened to fire them from their jobs or harm their children. The effort died because of white intimidation.

Lafayette and his wife, Colia, began holding meetings to educate people about voting, and by June as many as seven hundred people were attending them. Whites were so angry at their success that a group of them on June 12, 1963, beat up Lafayette. On the same night, Medgar Evers, a prominent black civil rights leader in Jackson, Mississippi, was shot to death at his home. And just a few months later, on September 15, four young girls— Addie Mae Collins, Denise McNair, Carole Robertson, and Cynthia

Wesley—were murdered when the Ku Klux Klan (KKK) bombed the Sixteenth Street Baptist Church in Birmingham, Alabama.

White violence did not stop the Selma voter drive. On October 7, 1963, SNCC organized a Freedom Day in which three hundred blacks lined up at the Dallas County Courthouse to register. Clark had a photographer take pictures of everyone in line. He then promised to show the photos to the protesters' employers to make the blacks afraid they would lose their jobs for trying to

The Ku Klux Klan bombed a Birmingham, Alabama, church in 1961, resulting in the deaths of four young girls.

register. Deputies arrested SNCC workers who carried signs that read "Register Now For Freedom," beat volunteers who tried to give sandwiches and drinks to people waiting in line, and roughed up reporters covering the protest.

Four Federal Bureau of Investigation (FBI) and two U.S. Justice Department attorneys who were present at the Freedom Day protest did nothing about the abuse. But the Justice Department in November filed a restraining order to stop Clark, other officials, and private citizens from interfering with black voting rights. In March 1964 a federal judge dismissed the suit by claiming no abuse of police powers had taken place. The failure of local federal judges or other public officials to help protect black rights in such cases was common in southern states. Thus, protesting remained the only option blacks had to win their rights.

Another Selma Confrontation

The SNCC voting effort in Selma in the first half of 1964 had consisted only of weekly mass meetings as blacks awaited the result of the request for a restraining order. But that changed on July 2 when the Civil Rights Act of 1964 went into effect. The law, which Congress had passed as the result of a new awareness of the plight of southern blacks due to media coverage of civil rights protests, was designed to end Jim Crow. It outlawed racial segregation in schools, the workplace, and facilities or businesses such as hotels or stores that served the public. It also banned unequal application of voter registration requirements.

When Selma blacks on July 4 tested the law, whites beat up several people who tried to enter the Wilby Theater to see a movie. And when four people tried to eat at the Thirsty Boy drive-in, police arrested them for trespassing. The next day blacks held a voter registration rally. But Clark, his deputies, and his "Sheriff's posse"—citizens who helped him harass protesters—used billy clubs and tear gas to break up the protest. On July 6 John Lewis led fifty blacks to the Selma courthouse. Clark angrily told Lewis he had come to Selma solely to cause trouble. Lewis responded by saying: "Sheriff, I may be an agitator, but I'm not an outsider. I grew up ninety miles from here. And we are going to stay here until these people are allowed to register."[25] Clark and his men then beat and arrested Lewis and other protesters.

SNCC leader John Lewis, in light coat, center, is beaten by Sheriff Jim Clark's deputies outside a Selma courthouse while demonstrating for black voting rights. He was later hospitalized with a skull fracture.

On July 9 federal judge James Hare issued an injunction forbidding public gatherings in Selma of more than three people for political purposes. Hare claimed he acted to ensure public safety, but the judge was known for making racist statements, and civil rights supporters felt his order was really aimed at stopping blacks from meeting and fighting for their rights. Hare's court order and Clark's brutal treatment of protesters highlighted the major obstacle southern blacks faced in their civil rights fight—the racist attitudes of public officials whom they had no voice in electing. When Clark was asked why so few blacks were registered to vote, he claimed it was "largely because of their [low] mental I.Q."[26] Hare once voiced an even more repellent racist view of blacks while discussing whether they should be allowed to vote. In words reminiscent of a nineteenth-century slave owner, Hare told a reporter: "You see, most of your Selma Negroes are descended from the Ebo and Angola tribes of Africa. You could never teach or trust an Ebo back in slave days, and even today I can spot their tribal characteristics. They have protruding heels, for instance."[27]

The Justice Department sought to overturn Hare's order and filed a complaint against Clark. But when the legal motions became stalled in the court system, Selma blacks seemed powerless to continue fighting for their rights. Even Lewis admitted that "by the end of [1965], our efforts in Selma had come practically to a standstill."[28] That changed when Martin Luther King Jr. decided to help Selma blacks gain the right to vote.

King Becomes Involved

In the fall of 1964, only 335 of Dallas County's 15,115 voting-age blacks were registered even though U.S. Justice Department attorney John Doar had been working through the courts to ease voting registration barriers. In August Doar had admitted that although "the litigation method of correction has been tried harder here than anywhere else in the south [blacks were still denied] the most fundamental of their constitutional rights—the right to vote."[29] The failure of both SNCC and the government to change the situation led Selma blacks to ask King for help. Boynton and several other residents visited King at his home in Atlanta when he returned home from Oslo, Norway, after accepting the Nobel Peace Prize on December 11, 1964, for his civil rights work.

King knew voting was the key to black equality and had already been thinking about fighting for that right in a city like Selma. In early December when Lyndon Baines Johnson held a White House reception for him after he received the peace prize, King had asked Johnson to introduce a voting rights bill. Johnson declined, claiming it was too soon after the 1964 Civil Rights Act: "I'm going to do it eventually, but I can't get a voting rights bill through in this session of Congress."[30]

Johnson's hesitation helped King decide to go to Selma when he was asked later that month. Another factor in his decision was the racist brutality Clark displayed toward blacks. In 1963 when King led civil rights protests in Birmingham, Alabama, police chief Eugene "Bull" Connor had used tear gas, fire hoses, and attack dogs on protesters. Newspaper and television stories about the brutality shocked the nation and helped convince Congress to pass the 1964 civil rights bill. King hoped Clark's brutal treatment of blacks could force Johnson and Congress to act more swiftly to protect black voting rights. King discussed

Jim Clark and Annie Lee Cooper

One of the most dramatic and violent encounters in the early voter registration protests in Selma, Alabama, was between Sheriff Jim Clark and Annie Lee Cooper. Protest leader John Lewis describes what happened on January 22, 1965:

> As Clark's men moved in and began pushing people aside, Mrs. Cooper—all 235 pounds of her—confronted him. "Ain't nobody scared around here," she said. Clark wasn't one to stand for backtalk, especially from a woman. He shoved Mrs. Cooper hard. But not hard enough. She came right back and punched the sheriff in the head, sending him reeling. Three deputies then grabbed Mrs. Cooper and wrestled her to the ground, where she kept flailing and kicking even as they held her down. Clark looked out of his mind with anger. He had his billy club out and looked as if he was about to hit her with it. Then he hesitated. You could see his mind clicking in, the realization that everyone was watching. Us. The reporters. The photographers. Everyone. ["I] wish you would hit me, you scum," she snapped at [Clark]. He then brought his billy club down on her head with a whack that was heard throughout the crowd gathered in the street. It took two pairs of handcuffs to hold Mrs. Cooper as she was taken away to jail, blood dripping from a wound over her right eye.

Quoted in Herb Boyd. *We Shall Overcome.* Naperville, IL: Sourcebooks, 2004, p. 191.

Annie Lee Cooper fights with Jim Clark's deputies as they attempt to take her into custody after Clark beat her with a billy club.

the rationale for that tactic in a book he wrote in 1967: "[Efforts] in a single city such as Birmingham or Selma produced situations that symbolized the evil everywhere and inflamed public opinion against it. Where the spotlight [of news coverage] illuminated the evil, a legislative remedy was soon obtained that applied everywhere."[31]

King decided to stage a series of protests that would showcase the plight of Selma blacks to the nation. He arranged to speak there on January 2, 1965, to kick off the protests. But even before King got there, white officials had learned he was coming and began preparing to deal with him.

White Selma Prepares for King

When Joseph Smitherman was elected Selma mayor in the fall of 1964, he knew dealing with civil rights protests would be one of the most difficult parts of his job. Years after the 1965 protests, this is how Smitherman described King's decision to come to Selma: "They picked Selma just like a movie producer would pick a set. You had the right ingredients."[32] Because Smitherman knew Clark's violent behavior could tarnish the city's image in the event of protests, the newly elected mayor created the new position of public safety director. Because the director would have authority over all law enforcement in Selma, it was an attempt to limit Clark's involvement in policing protests.

Smitherman appointed Wilson Baker to the new post. Baker was a former Selma police captain who had been teaching law enforcement at the University of Alabama–Tuscaloosa since he had lost a 1958 campaign for sheriff to Clark. Although Baker opposed black rights, he believed in doing it peacefully because he knew law enforcement violence helped the black cause.

In an attempt to keep King out of Selma, Smitherman sent Baker to Washington, D.C., in late December to meet with Burke Marshall, who headed the Justice Department's Civil Rights Division. Baker argued that violence would occur in Selma because King would inflame an already tense situation. In return for having King stay out of Selma, Baker promised that the city would make it easier for blacks to register and would stop using violence against protesters. Marshall immediately telephoned King to explain Baker's offer. When Marshall hung up, he told Baker

"They're coming to Selma. They already put too much work in on the project to turn back now."[33]

A few days later, King came to Selma to begin protests that would shock the nation and help blacks gain the right to vote.

King Comes to Selma

January 2 was an unusually cold winter day in Selma—it even snowed, which was rare in the Deep South. The Reverend Patrick Reese, president of the DCVL, was worried the cold and threat of being arrested would keep people from coming to hear King speak. But at 3 P.M. Brown's Chapel African Methodist Episcopal Church was packed with nine hundred people. For the first time in six months, Selma blacks broke the court order barring more than three blacks from assembling in one place for political purposes. Reese said "[Having] to arrest that number of people would have been a liability on the city to fit all those people in jail."[34] So instead of arresting people, police directed traffic so they could park their cars.

When King arrived, one of the twentieth century's most powerful orators did not disappoint the huge crowd. In an impassioned, eloquent speech punctuated by cries of "Amen" and "That's right!" from those listening, King said blacks would no longer allow southern whites to deny them the right to vote: "At the rate they are letting us register now, it will take a hundred and three years to register all of the fifteen thousand Negroes in Dallas County who are qualified to vote. We don't *have* that *long* to wait!" But King also warned Selma blacks they would have to fight hard for that right: "We must be ready to march; we must be willing to go to jail by the thousands. We will dramatize the situation to arouse the federal government [to action] by marching by the thousands to the place of registration. [We are] not on our knees begging for the ballot, *We are demanding the ballot*."[35]

After his speech, King went to Boynton's home to meet local leaders and plan strategy for the voter registration campaign. Although the protests would not begin for almost two weeks, King and Selma blacks were further emboldened two days later on January 4 when Johnson expressed his commitment to voting rights. In his State of the Union Address, Johnson promised

Martin Luther King Jr. came to Selma and spoke at the Brown Chapel African Methodist Episcopal Church on January 2, 1965. King told the packed church that blacks could no longer allow southern whites to deny them the right to vote.

to help African Americans win that right "through enforcement of the civil rights law and elimination of barriers to [voting]."[36]

Johnson's promise set the stage for the dramatic events in Selma.

Selma Blacks Protest

On Monday morning January 18, Selma blacks began their fight for equality by eating at seven whites-only restaurants to successfully test the 1964 Civil Rights Act. Then King and Lewis led four hundred people from Brown's Chapel to the Dallas County Courthouse. The city had refused blacks a parade permit. To avoid being arrested, they walked the nine blocks to the downtown area four abreast on sidewalks instead of marching as one group down the street. At the courthouse, a large group of whites who opposed black rights had gathered. Clark forced people who wanted to register to vote to stand in an alley in back of the courthouse. After waiting peacefully for several hours without having officials register anyone, they left.

No violence occurred at the courthouse, but it did later when King became the first black to stay at the Hotel Albert. While King was registering, Jimmie George Robinson of the National States

Young Protesters

———————————■———————————

Eight-year-old Sheyann Webb was one of the youngest protesters in Selma, Alabama, in 1965. Webb sang at rallies at Brown Chapel African Methodist Episcopal Church and participated in protests. On March 1, 1965, she was arrested while marching on the same day the Reverend Martin Luther King Jr. was arrested. Webb describes her arrest:

About three hundred students—most of them junior-high kids who were older than me—gathered at the church, began singing songs, and then started to march to the city hall. They carried signs about having the right to vote and about getting Dr. King out of jail. I went with them and before we got to the city hall [safety director Wilson] Baker got in front of us and announced that it was "time for you to go on home." He kept repeating that he didn't want us to be in trouble, that he wanted us to go home. Every time he'd say something, we'd listen, then start singing again so, finally, he announced that we were all to follow him, that we were under arrest. Everybody was laughing and clapping their hands then, and walked down the street behind him. They took our names down as we passed by the desk, and some of us were then told to go home. The others were jailed.

Sheyann Webb and Rachel West Nelson. *Selma, Lord, Selma: Childhood Memories of the Civil-Rights Days as Told to Frank Sikora*. Tuscaloosa: University of Alabama Press, 1980, pp. 61–62.

Rights Party, a racist group, asked King, "Could you step over here for just a minute?"[37] When King moved toward him, Robinson punched King in the head. Robinson was restrained by Lewis and another man, but police never charged him for attacking King.

Clark had restrained his violent tendencies in dealing with blacks that first day, but he displayed his brutish nature on Tuesday when blacks returned to the courthouse. Protesters refused to go to the rear of the building to wait to register as they had done on Monday because they felt that was demeaning. Clark and his deputies then ordered them off the courthouse sidewalk. When Boynton was slow to obey the order, Clark grabbed the fifty-four-year-old woman by the collar of her coat, dragged her down the street, and shoved her in a squad car. This is how Boynton described the incident: "[Clark] yelled to me, 'Where are you going. You all got to get in this line [in the alley].' Before I could gather my wits, he had left the [courthouse] steps and jumped behind me, grabbed me by the coat, propelled me around and then started shoving me down the street. I was stunned."[38]

The next day a photograph of the big sheriff forcing the small woman down the street was printed in the *New York Times* and *Washington Post* newspapers. News stories of the event explained that Boynton was one of sixty-seven people arrested for unlawful assembly for gathering at the courthouse, even though the U.S. Constitution allows people to gather to protest what they believe

Sheriff Jim Clark uses his billy club to intimidate a protester wanting to register to vote at the Dallas County Courthouse. When the protesters refused to be intimidated, they were all arrested.

are injustices. More protests and more arrests occurred during the next three days.

Perhaps the most significant march the first week was on Friday, January 22, by more than one hundred black teachers, a group that had shied away from past protests for fear of losing their jobs. They were met by Clark, deputies, and members of his "Sheriff's posse" armed with electric cattle prods and wooden billy clubs. The teachers tried to enter the courthouse three times but were shoved back down the building's thirteen green marble steps each time. Clark then ordered the teachers to leave or be arrested. They walked slowly back to Brown's Chapel in what was considered a triumph for teachers who had stood up for their rights even though they might be fired.

More Protests, More Arrests

When protests resumed on Monday, January 25, one of the participants was fifty-three-year-old Annie Lee Cooper. When deputies began shoving people off the courthouse steps, Cooper boldly declared, "Ain't nobody scared around here."[39] When Clark responded to her comment by shoving her hard, Cooper punched the sheriff twice, knocking him down. Two deputies then tried to wrestle Cooper to the ground, but the large, strong woman broke free and punched Clark again. When three deputies finally subdued Cooper, Clark hit her in the head with his billy club. Widespread national media coverage, including front-page newspaper photographs of Clark beating Cooper while she was restrained by deputies, again focused the nation's attention on the brutality southern blacks were enduring to win their rights.

One week later on Monday, February 1, King led 250 people from Brown's Chapel to the courthouse. Before the march began, King explained why the protests were important: "If Negroes could vote, there would be no Jim Clarks [and] our children would not be crippled by segregated schools."[40] When King had protesters march in one uninterrupted mass instead of in smaller groups, Baker told him he was violating the parade ordinance. King, who wanted to be arrested to heighten news coverage, refused to obey the order to stop the march. Even though Baker knew King's arrest would create a news sensation, he took King and several other protest leaders to jail.

Letter from a Selma Jail

When the Reverend Martin Luther King Jr. was arrested in Selma, Alabama, on February 1, 1965, he penned a letter that explains why African Americans were protesting there for the right to vote. This is part of that letter:

> When the King of Norway participated in awarding the Nobel Peace Prize to me [on December 11, 1964,] he surely did not think that in less than sixty days I would be in jail. [By] jailing hundreds of Negroes, the city of Selma, Alabama, has revealed the persisting ugliness of segregation to the nation and the world. When the Civil Rights Act of 1964 was passed many decent Americans were lulled into complacency because they thought the day of difficult struggle was over. Why are we in jail? [THIS] IS SELMA, ALABAMA. THERE ARE MORE NEGROES IN JAIL WITH ME [for protesting for their rights] THAN THERE ARE ON THE VOTING ROLLS. [When] reporters asked Sheriff [Jim] Clark if a woman defendant was married, he replied, "She's a n***** woman and she hasn't got a Miss or a Mrs. in front of her name." [We] are in jail simply because we cannot tolerate these conditions for ourselves or our nation.

Quoted in David J. Garrow. *Bearing the Cross: Martin Luther King Jr. and the Southern Christian Leadership Conference*. New York: HarperCollins, 1999, p. 386.

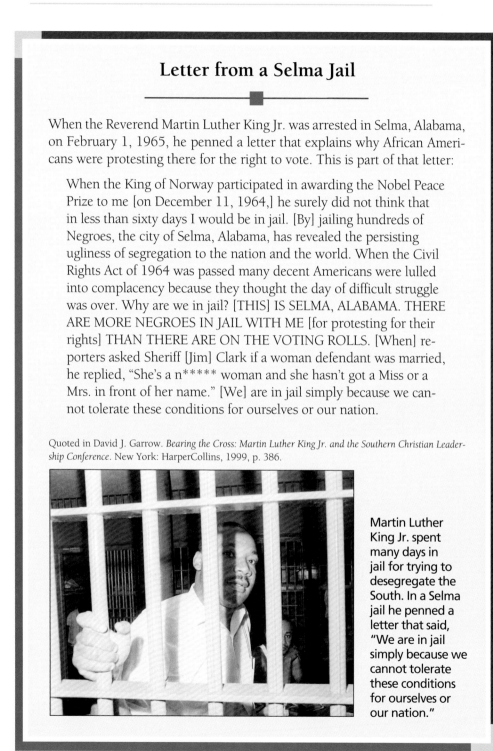

Martin Luther King Jr. spent many days in jail for trying to desegregate the South. In a Selma jail he penned a letter that said, "We are in jail simply because we cannot tolerate these conditions for ourselves or our nation."

The national news media heavily reported King's arrest. Newspapers, magazines, and television and radio stations also covered the arrests of nearly two thousand people over the next few days, including eight hundred schoolchildren, who marched to protest King's arrest. King used his time in jail to write a letter explaining why blacks were protesting in Selma. When his letter was printed in newspapers around the nation and reported widely in other forms of news media, it brought even more attention to the battle blacks were waging in Selma.

The dramatic events and resulting news coverage made protest leaders feel they were starting to achieve their goal, and SCLC official Andrew Young gleefully exclaimed, "Brother, we've got a movement going on."[41] Although many other people began using that phrase to show their pride in the protests, they had not accomplished anything yet. And they would soon find out how hard it was to defeat whites who desperately wanted to continue to deny them their rights.

Chapter Three

Bloody Sunday and a Symbolic March

Martin Luther King Jr. served four days in the Selma, Alabama, jail on the charge of leading a march without a proper parade permit. His release from jail on February 5, 1965, cheered everyone fighting to secure the right to vote for African Americans—so had two important events one day earlier. Federal judge Daniel Thomas on February 4 ordered Dallas County registrars to start processing new voters more quickly and to stop using a literacy test on government that was so hard it was an unfair roadblock to prospective voters. On that same day, Lyndon Baines Johnson backed the Selma voting drive. During a news conference, Johnson told reporters: "I should like to say that all Americans should be indignant when one American is denied the right to vote. The loss of that right to a single citizen undermines the freedom of every citizen. This is why all of us should be concerned with the efforts of our fellow Americans to register in Alabama."[42]

The cluster of positive actions, especially the support of the president, made protesters believe they were making progress toward their goal of securing the right to vote. But whites who feared that blacks would succeed started fighting back hard with one of their most powerful weapons—violence.

President Johnson expressed his support for the civil rights protesters in Selma, Alabama, and said that the loss of voting rights undermines the freedom of every American.

More Arrests and Violence

Monday, February 8, was one of only two days a month the Dallas County registrar's office, located in the courthouse in Selma, was open. When James Bevel of the SCLC entered the courthouse with prospective voters, Jim Clark tried to make him leave the building. "You're making a mockery out of justice,"[43] Clark told him. When Bevel argued that he had a right to help blacks register to vote, Clark repeatedly jabbed him with his billy club and then arrested him.

Clark was more brutal on February 10 while arresting 165 teenagers who had marched to the courthouse in support of black voting rights. Telling them sarcastically, "You wanted to march, didn't you?"[44] Clark had his deputies use cattle prods and billy clubs to force them on a brutal three-mile run. His deputies mocked and beat teenagers who could not keep up the fast pace.

The forced run terrified the teens, who were frightened something even worse could happen when it ended. Some young people were so scared and exhausted at the end of the run that they
threw up in ditches. Clark's men then took them to jail.

On Tuesday, February 16, the Reverend C.T. Vivian, an SCLC
leader already famous for fighting for black rights, led a group
of twenty-five people to the courthouse. Although the registrar's
office was not open, protesters went there to sign up to register
to vote in the future. When Clark and his deputies barred their
way, the Baptist minister told them they were as evil as the Ger-
man Nazis who followed Adolf Hitler's orders to murder millions
of people in World War II: "You're racists in the same way Hitler
was a racist."[45] Vivian's comment infuriated Clark, who ordered
a television cameraman, "Turn out that light or I'll shoot it out!"[46]
in an attempt to stop him from filming what would happen.
Clark then punched Vivian in the mouth. Vivian was arrested,
and through bleeding lips, accused Clark of beating people up to
deny them the right to vote. Cameras captured the punch despite
Clark's efforts, and it was shown in television news reports that
night.

Vivian was released from jail on Wednesday. The next night,
February 18, at Zion's Chapel Methodist Church in Marion, about
thirty miles west of Selma, Vivian spoke about his confrontation
with Clark. Vivian's speech preceded a planned march to protest the arrest of civil rights protesters in Marion. By the time the
meeting ended the church was surrounded by police, angry white
citizens, and Alabama state troopers led by Colonel Al Lingo, who
was infamous for his brutality toward blacks.

As nearly five hundred blacks left the church to begin marching
to the downtown area, officials ordered them to either go home or
back into the church. But John Lewis said that before protesters
had a chance to obey the order, "[the] street lights went out. As if
on cue, the police and troopers began beating the marchers while
a crowd of white onlookers leaped on the press, spraying the TV
camera lenses with paint [so they could not film what happened]
and assaulting the reporters. It was mayhem."[47]

When blacks fled for safety into the church and nearby businesses, law enforcement officers and citizens followed and bru-
tally beat them. After troopers used clubs in Mack's Cafe to

knock down eighty-two-year-old Cager Lee and his daughter, Viola Jackson, Jimmie Lee Jackson tried to protect his grandfather and mother. When Jackson fought trooper James Fowler, the officer shot the unarmed Jackson in the stomach. After King was informed of the violence, he sent a telegram to U.S. attorney general Nicholas Katzenbach claiming, "This situation can only encourage chaos and savagery in the name of law enforcement unless dealt with immediately."[48] Katzenbach contacted King and told him the Justice Department had already begun investigating the incident.

Sheriff Jim Clark grabs C.T. Vivian and denies him the right to register to vote. Clark then punched Vivian and arrested him for trying to exercise his constitutional rights.

Many Alabama whites were ecstatic over the Marion violence because they believed it had weakened the African American drive for voting rights. Some of them even rejoiced on February 26 when Jackson died in a hospital of the gunshot wound he had received. But what those jubilant whites did not know was that Jackson's death would trigger one of the most violent and important episodes in the struggle for black rights—a march that would become known in history as "Bloody Sunday."

A March for Jackson

On Sunday, February 28, Bevel spoke at Zion's Chapel Methodist Church in Marion during a memorial service honoring Jackson. His remarks included a Bible passage in which a queen named Esther was asked to go to an evil king and ask him to stop killing Jews. Bevel compared Alabama governor George Wallace to the king Esther went to see. Loudly shouting, "I must go see the king!" Bevel told mourners, "Be prepared to walk to Montgomery."[49] Bevel explained years later why he decided a mass march to the state capital in honor of Jackson would help blacks win the right to vote: "The whole point of walking from Selma to Montgomery is it takes you five or six days, which would give you the time to discuss in the nation, through papers, radio, and television and going around speaking, what the real issues were."[50]

Bevel even proposed carrying Jackson's casket to Montgomery to protest the injustice of his murder, but that did not materialize. Even though Bevel suggested the unique protest without consulting anyone else, the idea of a 54-mile (86.9km) march to the state capital quickly won support from King and other protest leaders. At Jackson's funeral in Marion on Wednesday, March 3, King claimed, "He was murdered by the brutality of every sheriff who practices lawlessness in the name of law."[51] Later in the day, King announced that the march Bevel proposed would be held on Sunday, March 7. When Wallace heard about the march, he angrily declared, "I'm not gonna have a bunch of n****** walking along a highway in the state as long as I'm governor."[52] To back up his promise, Wallace ordered the state patrol to stop marchers from ever leaving Selma.

On Saturday, March 6, about seventy Selma whites gathered at the Dallas County Courthouse to show their support for black voting and the next day's march. The Reverend Joseph Ellwanger said, "We consider it a shocking injustice that there are still counties in Alabama where there are no Negroes registered to vote and where Negroes have reason to fear hostility and harassment by public officials when they do try to register."[53] Whites who opposed black rights mocked the protesters and sang *Dixie*, a Civil War song that was an anthem for racists.

Although aides to Wallace had told Selma mayor Joe Smitherman there would be no violence, Selma safety director Wilson Baker told him he was crazy to believe the promise. Baker was so sure the march would result in an ugly exhibition of racism that he told Smitherman he would not allow Selma police to participate in enforcing Wallace's order to stop the march. Smitherman agreed. That meant marchers would be met by Clark, his deputies and "Sheriff's posse," state troopers commanded by Major John Cloud, and white citizens who gathered to watch the protest.

Pettus Bridge

On Sunday, March 7, hundreds of people gathered for the march at Brown Chapel African Methodist Episcopal Church and were surprised that King was not there. King had been in Selma the day before but had told protest leaders he wanted the march postponed until Monday so he could tend to his pastoral duties at Ebenezer Baptist Church in Atlanta, where he lived. But when so many people showed up for the march, protest leaders telephoned King, and he agreed with them that the march should proceed. His absence from the historic protest is considered one of the few mistakes King made while fighting for civil rights. In his absence, the march was led by SCLC leader Hosea Williams and Lewis, who headed SNCC. Even though SNCC opposed the march because its members felt it would fail, the Alabama native volunteered to march because he believed it was the right thing to do.

About 12:30 P.M., Williams and Lewis led some six hundred people from the chapel to the Edmund Pettus Bridge. The bridge arched high over the Alabama River and ended in highway U.S. 80, which led east out of Selma. When Williams and Lewis got to the bridge's high point, they saw a wall of troopers, deputies, and whites lined up shoulder-to-shoulder across the four lanes of U.S.

Jimmie Lee Jackson

On February 18, 1965, Jimmie Lee Jackson was shot by an Alabama State Trooper in Marion, Alabama. His death was a catalyst for the march by blacks from Selma to Montgomery just a few weeks later. Jackson was shot after he and other blacks, including his mother Viola and grandfather Cager Lee, had taken refuge in Mack's Cafe to escape troopers breaking up a nighttime march. Historian Charles E. Fager describes what happened:

> The troopers came after them, clubs swinging, splitting scalps and smashing ribs as they advanced. [The] troopers came inside, smashed all the light within reach and began clubbing the people indiscriminately. When one hit Viola Jackson and knocked her screaming to the floor, Jimmie Lee lunged at him. The trooper struck him across the face [and] then a trooper picked him up and slammed him against a cigarette machine while another trooper [James Fowler] drew his pistol and calmly shot Jackson point blank in the stomach. Jimmie didn't realize he had been shot until a few moments later, because the troopers continued beating him and the others unmercifully. Pulling himself up again from the floor, he ran blindly out of the door of the cafe, clutching his stomach [but] more troopers were waiting outside and he was struck again and again [until] he finally collapsed bleeding on the sidewalk.

Charles E. Fager. *Selma 1965: The March That Changed the South*. New York: Charles Scribner's Sons, 1974, p. 74.

An estimated 700 mourners follow the hearse bearing the body of Jimmie Lee Jackson to the cemetery. Jackson's brutal death would inspire the March to Montgomery.

80 at the bottom of the bridge. Seeing that their way was blocked, Williams said he could not swim. He then anxiously asked Lewis if he could swim, to which Lewis replied, "I can't either and I'm sure we're gonna end up in that river."[54] They both believed the massed whites might not only stop them from going forward but violently throw them off the bridge.

When the peaceful, unarmed marchers, including women and children, neared the bottom of the bridge, Cloud told them they had two minutes to turn around and go back to Brown Chapel. But after just one minute, Cloud gave an order to attack them.

Bloody Sunday

Lewis, who was in the front row of marchers, was the first marcher bloodied that day. He describes how a trooper knocked him down with a billy club: "Without a word, he swung his club against the left side of my head. I didn't feel any pain, just the thud of the blow and my legs giving way. I raised an arm—a reflex motion—as I curled up [to protect himself] and then the same trooper hit me again [and Lewis was knocked unconscious]."[55]

After Lewis was felled with a fractured skull, a line of troopers waded into the rows of marchers, beating anyone in their path, including Amelia Boynton, with billy clubs. "One trooper told me to run. I just gave him a dirty look," Boynton said. "He hit me. The second time he said 'Run,' he hit me at the base of my neck and I fell unconscious."[56] Frightened protesters began running to escape the violence. Among them was Sheyann Webb, who had been arrested on February 1 with other children while protesting King's arrest. At first, Sheyann did not know what was happening because she was too short to see anything over the people surrounding her: "I heard all this screaming [and I saw people] running and stumbling back toward us and some of them were crying out and somebody yelled, 'Oh, God they're killing us!'"[57] Sheyann then began running with everyone else.

People fled not only from the beatings but yellow and white clouds of tear gas troopers fired that stung their eyes and made it hard to breathe. The tear gas washed over protesters who had been beaten to the ground, those who were trying to help the injured, or those who were simply kneeling in prayer. Boynton, lying unconscious, nearly suffocated from gas before someone carried her

An Alabama state trooper approaches an unconscious woman as mounted troopers prepare to attack civil rights protesters at the Pettus Bridge on Bloody Sunday, March 7, 1965.

off the bridge. Members of Clark's posse on horses added another frightening element to the attack when they charged marchers. They used their horses, bullwhips, and rubber hoses wrapped in barbed wire to force marchers off the bridge.

The bridge was quickly cleared, but troopers, deputies, posse members, and whites pursued the protesters. They chased and beat people through Selma's streets all the way back to Brown Chapel, with some of them shouting nastily, "Get the hell out of town! We want all the n****** off the streets!"[58] When one marcher took refuge in the First Baptist Church, posse members followed him and threw him through a stained glass window that depicted Jesus as the Good Shepherd.

Seventeen marchers including Lewis were hospitalized and seventy more men, women, and children required emergency medical treatment. The ugly scenes of violence on the day that became known as "Bloody Sunday" quickly found their way to

A Little Girl Remembers

Eight-year-old Sheyann Webb was perhaps the youngest marcher during Bloody Sunday. She explains what happened to her on March 7, 1965:

> I saw those horsemen coming toward me and they rode right through the cloud of tear gas. Some of them had clubs, others had ropes or whips, which they swung about them like they were driving cattle. I just turned and ran [but] the tear gas got me; it burned my nose first and then got my eyes. I was blinded by tears. So I began running and not seeing where I was going. [Then] somebody was dragging me under the arms and lifting me up and running. The horses went by and I kept waiting to get trampled on or hit, but they went on by and I guess they [the riders] were hitting at somebody else. And I looked up and saw it was Hosea Williams who had me and he was running but we didn't seem to be moving, and I kept kicking my legs in the air, trying to speed up, and I shouted at him, "Put me down! You can't run fast enough with me!" But he held on until we were off the bridge and down on Broad Street and let me go. I didn't stop running until I got home.

Sheyann Webb and Rachel West Nelson. *Selma, Lord, Selma: Childhood Memories of the Civil-Rights Days as Told to Frank Sikora*. Tuscaloosa: University of Alabama Press, 1980, p. 97

Sheyan Webb was an eyewitness to the violence perpetrated by Alabama state troopers and Dallas County sheriff's deputies on the Bloody Sunday demonstrators.

national television. One television network even interrupted the film *Judgment at Nuremberg* early that evening to show video of what happened.

News stories and filmed reports of the brutality shocked the nation and the world. Smitherman later explained the impact that the dramatic images created: "When that beating happened at the foot of the bridge, it looked like war. That went all over the country. And the people, the wrath of the nation came down on us."[59]

King Demands Another March

People across the United States were outraged over the brutal force law enforcement officials had wielded against people who were peacefully protesting for a right they were being wrongfully denied. Thousands of people marched in demonstrations in scores of cities in support of the fight southern blacks were waging to be able to vote. Many newspapers, even some in the South, also condemned the violence. Most important, Bloody Sunday pushed Congress and Johnson to help blacks secure the vote. Johnson issued a statement that condemned "the brutality with which a number of Negro citizens of Alabama were treated when they sought to dramatize their deep and sincere interest in attaining the precious right to vote."[60] Johnson also vowed to introduce a voting rights bill in Congress the following week.

When King learned what had happened, he decided that blacks needed to stage a second march immediately to show that such racist violence could not stop blacks from seeking their rights. He scheduled it for Tuesday, March 9, and said he would lead it. King also decided to utilize the moral force of white members of the clergy from around the nation who supported black rights. King sent telegrams to about two hundred ministers that invited them to join this second march: "In the vicious maltreatment of defenseless citizens of Selma, where old women and young children were gassed and clubbed at random, we have witnessed an eruption of the disease of racism which seeks to destroy all Americans. No American is without responsibility. Join me in Selma for a ministers' march to Montgomery."[61]

The response to King's telegram was overwhelming, and more than 250 white clergymen and 200 other whites who backed black civil rights began heading for Selma. On Monday, SCLC attorneys also asked federal judge Frank M. Johnson in Montgomery to prohibit Alabama officials from interfering with the march. Johnson was sympathetic toward blacks but asked King to postpone the march until after he could hold a hearing on the request on Thursday. In addition, Governor Wallace stated he would not allow another march, which meant violence was again possible if protesters attempted to go to Montgomery on Tuesday.

Judge Johnson's request created a difficult situation for King, and a confusing series of events followed. King on early Monday night met with other leaders to discuss the judge's request. SNCC leader James Forman said King and the other leaders agreed to honor the request and not march. But after the meeting when King went to a rally at Brown Chapel, he became swept up in the emotions of the hundreds of people there and told them the march would go on as planned. His surprise announcement forced protest leaders to meet again to decide what to do. By 4 A.M. they had all agreed to go ahead with the march.

On Tuesday morning the judge issued a restraining order barring the protest, which he had promised to do. That put King in a difficult spot because he did not want to anger a judge who in the past had been sympathetic toward the black fight for civil rights. Additionally, President Johnson had asked King to stop the march, and King did not want to offend a president who had already done so much to help blacks. King's reluctance to anger powerful government officials sympathetic to the black cause led King to agree to a compromise with local and state officials. King agreed that protesters would march to the bridge, pray, and then turn back. The problem was that neither King nor other leaders made the compromise public.

A Symbolic March

On Tuesday afternoon nearly two thousand people gathered at Brown's Chapel. When King addressed them he boldly proclaimed "I do not know what lies ahead of us. There may be beatings, jailings, and tear gas. But I would rather die on the highways of Alabama than make a butchery of my conscience."[62] Shortly after 2:30 P.M., King led them out of the church to the Pettus Bridge.

At the bottom of the bridge the marchers were once again met by Alabama state troopers and county deputies. When Cloud or-

As the result of a compromise that had been worked out between King and other leaders, King decided to hold this prayer vigil at Brown Chapel on March 9 rather than march to Montgomery and incite violence again.

dered the protesters to stop, King claimed they had a right to march. When Cloud repeated the order, King asked only if they could pray. Four people prayed, including the Reverend Ralph Abernathy. The SCLC leader declared, "We come to present our bodies as a living sacrifice. We don't have much to offer, but we do have our bodies, and we lay them on the altar today."[63] After the prayers, the marchers sang the civil rights anthem "We Shall Overcome."

But instead of marching forward as everyone expected when the song ended, King led them back across the bridge to Brown's Chapel. There King told newsmen about the compromise and admitted to them that when the march began, "We knew we would not get to Montgomery."[64] Most marchers were shocked and confused when they turned back because they had not known about the prearranged deal. One was the Reverend Orloff Miller, a white Unitarian minister who had traveled from Boston to march with King. When King turned back, Miller said "I was aghast. What is going on? Are we not going through with this confrontation?"[65] SNCC worker Silas Norman was more angry than confused about the situation, saying, "I felt that we had been betrayed."[66] Some SNCC workers were so angry that they left Selma and began working on other civil rights projects.

During a meeting that night at Brown's Chapel, many people criticized King for not challenging Cloud's troopers and trying

A Secret Compromise

The Reverend Martin Luther King Jr. shocked and angered many of the two thousand people with him on March 9, 1965, when he unexpectedly headed back across the Pettus Bridge into Selma, Alabama. Thus the second attempt to march from Selma to Montgomery became only a symbolic gesture instead of a real effort to defy Alabama state troopers by going to Alabama's state capital. King, however, was honoring a compromise with state and local officials that had been worked out by LeRoy Collins. The former Florida governor headed the federal Community Relations Service, which mediated problems between blacks and whites. Collins arrived in Selma early Tuesday to tell King that President Johnson wanted him to postpone the march. When King refused, Collins then met with Dallas County sheriff Jim Clark and state trooper Colonel Al Lingo to ask them to refrain from more violence. The three agreed that blacks could march to the bridge, pray, and then go back to Selma. Clark and Lingo would not allow blacks to go further because Governor George Wallace had banned such marches. Collins also knew federal judge Frank M. Johnson would issue an injunction against the march Tuesday while he considered overturning Wallace's ban. Collins met again with King, but his response seemed vague; even Collins did not know what he would do. King later decided to honor the compromise and wait for Judge Johnson to clear the way for a legal march.

to continue the march all the way to Montgomery. SNCC worker Ivanhoe Donaldson reminded everyone, "Within the [civil
rights] movement, we are a family. Arguments take place in any
family."[67] That was the attitude most people took. So when King
declared the march a victory simply because blacks had shown
they were still willing to fight for their rights, it was generally
agreed that something good had taken place that day. But blacks
and their white supporters also knew they had to keep fighting to
reach their goal of being able to vote. And that made them more
determined than ever to complete the march to Montgomery.

Chapter Four

A Joyous March to Montgomery

One positive outcome of the failed attempt to march to Montgomery, Alabama, on March 9, 1965, was that no one was injured during the confrontation with law enforcement officials at the Pettus Bridge. But some blacks claimed that happened because so many protesters were white. James Forman said law enforcement officials did not attack marchers because "they don't beat white people. It's Negroes they beat and kill."[68] Only hours later, Forman's cynical claim was proven wrong. That night three white Unitarian ministers who had come to Selma to march with blacks—Orloff Miller, Clark Olsen, and James Reeb—ate dinner at Walker's Cafe, a restaurant in the city's black area. While walking back to Brown Chapel African Methodist Episcopal Church, three white men recognized them as civil rights supporters. The men were angry and called the ministers "n******" because they had marched with blacks. Olsen describes how the men then attacked them: "I perceived one of them swing [a] club-type thing at Jim Reeb's head, hitting him over his left ear. Jim fell to the ground. Orloff Miller dropped to the ground per instructions [about protecting themselves from violence]. And I, having not gotten those instructions, ran away."[69]

One man chased Olsen and struck him several times with his fists. The two other whites hit and kicked Miller but not with the club or metal pipe used on Reeb. When the whites left, Olsen and Miller carried Reeb to safety. Reeb was hospitalized and died two days later of a skull fracture. The murder of a white minister from Boston seemed to shock and infuriate the nation more than the death of Jimmie Lee Jackson and led to many demonstrations

Reverend Jim Reeb, along with fellow Unitarian ministers Orloff Miller and Clark Olsen, were attacked by a group of white men, and Reeb was bludgeoned to death. The murder infuriated the nation.

around the country against such violence. SNCC's Stokely Carmichael claimed Reeb's death was considered more monstrous than Jackson's because he was white. Whether predominantly white America thought that way or not, Reeb's death further dramatized the voting rights campaign. It seemed to make many whites, from private citizens to members of Congress, more sympathetic toward the cause of civil rights.

Waiting for a Ruling

The day after Reeb was attacked, hundreds of people tried to march from Brown's Chapel to the Dallas County Courthouse to protest the attack. They were stopped after several blocks by city police, Alabama state troopers, and Jim Clark's "Sheriff's posse." Joseph Smitherman and Wilson Baker asked marchers to turn back because they feared more violence from racist whites who had gathered in Selma to oppose blacks. The Reverend L.L. Anderson of Tabernacle Baptist Church responded, "Mr. Mayor, we are not here to rebel against your order [but] we feel we have no alternative but to offer our bodies as a living sacrifice."[70] Anderson began introducing representatives of various religions who had come from around the country to support Selma blacks, including a group of Catholic nuns from St. Louis. For several hours members of the group prayed, sang songs, and explained why they supported black rights. They then headed back to Brown's Chapel.

Reeb died the next day, Thursday, March 11. That was also the day Frank M. Johnson began his hearing on the SCLC request to stop local and state officials from interfering with the march to Montgomery. Johnson heard testimony for three days from the parties involved and then went to work on his decision about the march. Because law officials continued to enforce Johnson's injunction against marching, Selma blacks and their white supporters were unable to mount any significant protests. But that did not mean no progress was being made in the fight for the black vote.

Lyndon Baines Johnson, congressmen, and U.S. Justice Department officials began working out details of a voting act to help southern blacks vote. The president also tried to remove a major roadblock to a march to Montgomery by meeting with George Wallace in Washington, D.C., on Saturday, March 13. In a three-hour meeting, Johnson tried to get Wallace to help him end violence against blacks and their white supporters. Wallace later jokingly admitted Johnson had been so persuasive that "if I'd stayed in there much longer, he'd have had me comin' out for civil rights."[71]

On March 10 people marched to the Dallas County Courthouse to protest the beating of James Reeb. Sheriff Clark's "Sheriff's posse," under threat of more violence, forced them back to Brown's Chapel.

In a news conference after the meeting, Johnson told reporters that he would ask Congress in two days to pass a bill to remove all barriers stopping southern blacks from voting. In his nationally televised address to Congress on Monday, March 15, Johnson eloquently explained why the Voting Rights Act of 1965 had to be passed: "Their cause must be our cause, too. Because it's not just Negroes, but it's really all of us who must overcome the crippling legacy of bigotry and injustice. And, we *shall* overcome."[72] Johnson's use of the black battle cry "We shall overcome" was the most memorable part of his speech. C.T. Vivian and other protest leaders who were watching the address were deeply moved when Johnson used a phrase sacred to blacks. Vivian said, "We all cheered. I looked over toward Martin [Luther King Jr.] and a tear ran down his cheek."[73]

Two days later on Wednesday, March 17, Judge Johnson finally issued his ruling on the request to march to Montgomery. He granted blacks the right to march and ordered state and local officials in Alabama not to interfere with them. The judge said the marchers deserved the right to protest for voting rights because the state and local government had for so long denied them a citizen's most important right: "It seems basic to our principles that the extent of the right to assemble, demonstrate and march peaceably, along the highways and streets in an orderly manner, should be commensurate [equal] with the enormity of the wrongs that are being protested and petitioned against. In this case, the wrongs are enormous."[74]

His ruling set the scene for the most joyous, historic protest in the long battle blacks had waged for their rights.

Preparing for the March

The march was immediately scheduled for Sunday, March 21, just two weeks after Bloody Sunday. Although John Lewis was delighted the march could go on, he knew it would take a lot of work to make it possible. Lewis even admitted in his autobiography that blacks on March 7 had not been prepared to march all the way to Montgomery: "There had been nowhere near the preparations and logistics necessary to move that many people in an orderly manner down fifty-four miles of highway."[75]

A federal marshal reads a court order trying to halt the march at Selma to a group including Martin Luther King Jr. and Andrew Young (with his arms crossed). Young was responsible for organizing hundreds of volunteers along the route to Montgomery.

One of the first tasks was to pick the people who would march to Montgomery. Although thousands of people wanted to hike the 54 miles (86.9km) from Selma to Montgomery along U.S. 80, Judge Johnson had restricted the number of marchers to three hundred for most of the time it would take to walk there. He imposed that limit because the highway was four lanes wide heading out of Selma but narrowed a few miles later to only two lanes for most of the rest of the way east to Montgomery. Johnson believed that if too many people marched, there would be safety concerns because traffic still had to keep moving on the highway. Because so few people would be allowed to walk, protest leaders tried to select a broad representation of those who wanted to march. The lucky ones who were chosen—they became known as Freedom Marchers—included veteran civil rights leaders such as Lewis,

Selma natives active in previous protests, and members of various groups that had supported the march.

Protest organizers also had to figure out how to care for people during the four days of the march. That included providing marchers with food, portable bathrooms, shelter each night while they slept, and emergency medical care. Andrew Young was one of the protest leaders in charge of hundreds of volunteers who provided those services. He said, "The march from Selma to Montgomery, from my perspective, was a job. There was absolutely nothing romantic about it."[76] Many of those who wanted to march but were not chosen volunteered for the scores of jobs available to help the march proceed smoothly.

To ensure the safety of the marchers against racial violence, President Johnson deployed eighteen hundred Alabama National Guardsmen, two thousand U.S. Army troops, and hundreds of FBI and U.S. marshals along the route to Montgomery.

One of the main concerns facing organizers was how to protect people from racist whites who objected to the march. When Wallace refused to help, claiming it was too expensive, President Johnson provided the needed security. He ordered eighteen hundred members of the Alabama National Guard, two thousand U.S. Army troops, and hundreds of FBI agents and U.S. marshals to guard marchers.

The March Begins

On Sunday, March 21, about thirty-two hundred blacks and whites congregated for the historic march at Brown's Chapel. The crowd included notables like Ralph Bunche, an African American who had helped found the United Nations; author James Baldwin; and folksinger Joan Baez. They heard King, in the dramatic cadences of the brilliant orator he was, explain the importance of the march that was about to begin: "This is one of the greatest demonstrations for human rights in history. We have waited, have waited for freedom. We are tired of waiting. Walk together, children. Don't you get weary, and it will lead us to the promised land. And Alabama will be a new Alabama, and America will be a new America."[77]

Led by King and other march leaders wearing flower leis provided by a group from Hawaii, the huge crowd set out from Brown Chapel for the third and final time. There was no violence, but whites gathered near the church shouted racist remarks and obscenities such as "I hate n******!" at blacks and "Yankee trash go home!"[78] to whites. Marchers paused briefly at the Pettus Bridge, the site of such horror two weeks earlier, and then continued toward Montgomery.

The first day's march was only seven miles. Because only three hundred people would continue the second day, marchers dropped out along the way and either walked or were driven back to Selma. The first nightly encampment was on the farm of David Hall, an African American father of eight. The three hundred marchers spent the night in a field, sleeping on air mattresses in large tents. Marchers had eaten bag lunches during the day, but that night they had spaghetti and pork and beans. The food had been cooked in Selma, transported to marchers by car, and served from eight large galvanized garbage cans. Small generators provided lighting, and there were portable bathrooms for sanitation.

On March 21, 1965, Martin Luther King Jr. led a half-mile-long line of demonstrators across the Edmund Pettus bridge to start the march to Montgomery.

The first night of the march was cold; temperatures dipped below freezing, and even donated blankets failed to keep marchers warm. The Reverend Richard Leonard of New York City's Community Church, the nation's largest Unitarian congregation, admitted the next morning to a reporter, "I froze and you can quote me." But Leonard said he did not mind the bitter conditions: "I found myself. Suffering intensified determination [to support blacks]."[79] Other marchers would express similar emotions in the next few days as they tiredly trudged toward Montgomery.

Marching to Montgomery

Among the whites who set out for Montgomery on March 22 were clergymen like Leonard and Father Sherill Smith, a Catholic priest from San Antonio, Texas. When Smith was asked why he traveled to Selma for the march, he admitted it was hard to explain. He finally answered, "All I know is that I just had to put my feet on this highway, and I just had to walk."[80] Also there was Jim Letherer of Saginaw, Michigan, who hobbled along on crutches. When asked why a northern white man was marching, Letherer said, "I believe in brotherhood. My handicap is not that I have only one leg. It is that I cannot do more to help these people vote."[81]

The proudly marching African Americans included not only famous leaders like King and Ralph Abernathy but also many average people. Selma native Marie Foster remembers how difficult it was to keep walking every day for five days to get to Montgomery. "Ooooh, I would be so tired by the end of every day,"[82] she said. And there was eighty-two-year-old Cager Lee, whose grandson Jimmie Lee Jackson had been killed in Marion during an attempted nighttime march. Lee walked much of the route despite age and infirmity and while he shuffled along could be heard saying over and over, "Just got to tramp some more."[83] His intrepid marching inspired younger people who were also growing weary.

Moving at a pace of about 2 miles (3.2km) per hour, the column of marchers walking three abreast was preceded by two Alabama Highway Patrol cars, four unmarked cars carrying federal officials, a U.S. Army jeep, and a truck transporting video and still-camera photographers recording the march. The marchers were followed by ambulances, two more army jeeps, a communications van, a truck with portable bathrooms, and cars loaded with reporters.

As marchers inched toward Montgomery, helicopters and airplanes flew overhead as part of the security measures to protect them. Armed soldiers were also posted fifty feet apart along the entire route with larger groups of them at each intersection. Lewis, a victim of racist violence on Bloody Sunday and several other times in civil rights protests, marveled at the military escort. But he also found it ironic that peaceful protesters needed so much protection: "It was almost a contradiction, really, that these unarmed few nonviolent [civil rights] soldiers were being guarded by men with guns and riding jeeps."[84] The heavy security prevented any violence, but whites standing along the highway or passing in vehicles shouted obscenities at marchers. That was in sharp contrast to the warm reception marchers got from African Americans who lined the highway to honor the marchers. On the second day, Monday, March 22, as marchers neared

Whites Showed Their Hatred

Participants in the march from Selma to Montgomery were protected from physical harm by soldiers and law enforcement officers. But as journalist Simeon Booker notes in his May 1965 article for *Ebony* magazine, all along the 54-mile route (87km), racist whites showed their hatred of blacks and the white supporters of civil rights through words, gestures, and signs. The outpouring of racism started when the marchers left Selma for Montgomery on March 21, 1965. After marchers crossed the Pettus Bridge, assembled whites began berating them:

> Profanity—blue with hatred—sounded even from chubby-faced kids. There were gnarled fists, spit, grimaces and crudely written signs. Ironically, the targets for abuse were not Drs. King and Bunche, or the hundreds of other Negroes: the newly hated were the whites—the pure-faced nuns, the clerics with high collars, the energetic college students, and the occasional beatnik. It was a rude awakening to the visiting whites and it took the words of a freedom song with the phrase "black and white together" to soothe hurt feelings. Instances of love vs. hate dotted the atmosphere as much as the Confederate flags waving in hands. A woman shouted, "scum of the earth" and a nun answered "I love you." A thin, scraggly dressed man hollered "n***** lover" and a white pastor smiled and called him "brother." A child barely able to walk spat hard against the ground. At the catchiest hate calls, the state troopers grinned in delight, encouraging the gang to become more creative in damning the "outside agitators."

Simeon Booker. "50,000 March on Montgomery." *Ebony*, May 1965, p. 55.

Whites showed their hatred of blacks and white supporters through their words, gestures, and signs all along the fifty-four-mile route to Montgomery.

Moving at a pace of two miles an hour through the rain, the marchers, pictured here near the halfway point, made their way to Montgomery.

Trickem Forks, seventy-year-old Mary Jane Jackson was one of scores of blacks anxiously awaiting their arrival. "Lordy! Look at 'em come,"[85] said Jackson, who was thrilled when she got to kiss King. When King asked Trickem Forks blacks if they were going to register to vote, they all said yes.

On the second night marchers camped on the Rosie Steele farm. Steele said when protest leaders asked if they could use her farm for the night, "I couldn't afford to turn them down. If the president can take a stand, I guess I can too."[86] The seventy-year-old African American widow expressed the hope that she would live long enough to one day be able to vote herself.

A Party in Montgomery

On Tuesday morning, March 23, King left to give a speech in Cleveland but promised to be back on Thursday when marchers would reach Montgomery. Rain moved in Tuesday and soaked marchers even though they donned raincoats or covered themselves with plastic sheeting. For marchers, it was a tiring day as they walked 17 miles (27.4km) though a low, wet area known as the Big Swamp. Marchers kept themselves from getting discouraged by singing a walking tune with the lyrics: "What do you want? . . . Freedom! . . . When do you want it? . . . Now! . . . Where are we going? . . . Montgomery!"

That night marchers slept in a field owned by A.G. Gaston, a black businessman from Birmingham, Alabama. Bruce Hartford was a member of the security detail of volunteers who helped soldiers and law enforcement officers protect marchers. He said the rain turned the field into a sea of mud: "The campsite was just deep in mud and people were trying to sleep in mud [and] everybody was miserable. I mean, nobody got any sleep. Being in mud is horrible."[87]

The sun came up on Wednesday, March 24, to cheer and warm everyone up. When U.S. 80 widened to four lanes at the end of the Lowndes County border, hundreds and then thousands of people began joining the march. The new marchers had been ferried there by bus and car from Selma and nearby Montgomery. Judge Johnson's order allowed more marchers on the wider section of highway because cars could be confined to the other two lanes of the road.

Marchers reached the state capitol in Montgomery on March 25. As the march neared Montgomery many thousands of people joined.

A Joyous Celebration

The giant rally on March 25, 1965, in Montgomery, Alabama, was symbolic of how far African Americans had come in a century. As one of the most important cities of the Confederate States during the Civil War that began in 1861, it was a symbol of slavery and racism. Now, blacks were demanding full citizenship in the United States of America. This is scholar Stephen B. Oates's description of the final phase of the march:

> [Twenty-five thousand] people passed the Jefferson Davis Hotel, with a huge Rebel flag draped across its front, and Confederate Square. There were hundreds of Negroes from the Montgomery area, one crying [out] "This is the day! This is the day!" There was a plump, bespectacled white woman who carried a basket in one arm and a sign in the other: "Here is one native Selman for freedom and justice." [Like] a conquering army, they surged up Dexter Avenue to the capitol building, with Confederate and Alabama flags snapping over its dome. It was up Dexter Avenue that Jefferson Davis's first inaugural parade [as president of the Confederacy] had moved, and it was in the portico of the capitol that Davis had taken his oath of office as President of the slave-based Confederacy. Now, more than a century later, Alabama Negroes—most of them descendants of slaves—stood massed at the same statehouse, singing "We Have Overcome" with state troopers and the statue of Davis himself looking on.

Stephen B. Oates. "The Week the World Watched Selma." *American Heritage*, June/July 1982. www .americanheritage.com/articles/magazine/ah/1982/4/1982_4_48.shtml.

The campsite that night was the City of St. Jude, a Catholic facility, including a church and medical building, dedicated to helping poor blacks. By the time the day's march ended, the number of walkers numbered in the thousands and included King. That night, a crowd of twenty thousand people gathered for a four-hour "Stars of Freedom" rally featuring celebrity entertainers such as Harry Belafonte; Tony Bennett; Sammy Davis Jr.; Joan Baez; Peter, Paul and Mary; and Dick Gregory. They performed on a makeshift stage of coffins borrowed from a black funeral home.

The joyous celebration would pale in comparison to what happened the next day when fifty thousand people marched in Alabama's capital to demand that blacks be allowed to vote. The rally would be the largest civil rights protest ever held in the South.

Montgomery at Last!

There were new concerns over violence the morning of Thursday, March 25, because of a death threat against King. The civil rights icon had lived with such threats ever since he had led the Montgomery bus boycott a decade earlier. King, as usual, ignored the threat and said he would lead the march. To make it harder for someone to shoot King, protest leaders surrounded him with look-alikes wearing the same style blue suit he always wore. Thus, pictures of the final march into Montgomery show many blue-suited men leading the way. Right behind the blue suits came the three hundred Freedom Marchers, who wore orange vests to signify their special status.

The huge throng of black and white marchers proceeded joyously down Montgomery's main streets to the state capitol for the celebratory rally. They passed through Confederate Square, an area where blacks had once been sold as slaves. Many whites who watched from sidewalks and nearby buildings were angered or intimidated by the size of the huge crowd. When marchers arrived at the capitol, Wallace refused to come out and receive a petition demanding blacks be allowed to vote. Instead, the governor watched the rally from his office by peeking out from behind venetian blinds. Wallace had joked about the proposed march and claimed it would fail, but even he admitted to an aide, "That's quite a crowd out there."[88]

The highlight of the speeches and songs that day was King's speech. In one of his most impassioned and powerful speeches, King explained that southern whites had denied blacks the right to vote so they could continue to deny them other rights and dominate them politically, economically, and socially. Said King: "Our whole campaign in Alabama has been centered around the right to vote. In focusing the attention of the nation and the world today on the flagrant denial of the right to vote, we are exposing the very origin, the root cause, of racial segregation in the Southland."[89]

Another Historic Speech

The Reverend Martin Luther King Jr. was one of the twentieth century's most eloquent speakers. His speech on March 25, 1965, was one of the most powerful he ever delivered. In this excerpt, King tells blacks they have to keep fighting for their rights:

> [We] are on the move and no wave of racism can stop us. [The] burning of our churches will not deter us. The bombing of our homes will not dissuade us [and the] beating and killing of our clergymen and young people will not divert us. [We] are on the move now. Like an idea whose time has come, not even the marching of mighty armies can halt us. We are moving to the land of freedom. Let us therefore continue our triumphant march to the realization of the American dream. Let us march on segregated housing [and] march on segregated schools until every vestige of segregated and inferior education becomes a thing of the past. [Let] us march on poverty until no American parent has to skip a meal so that their children may eat. [Let] us march on ballot boxes until the Wallaces of our nation tremble away in silence [and] until brotherhood becomes more than a meaningless word in an opening prayer, but the order of the day on every legislative agenda.

Martin Luther King Jr. "Our God Is Marching On!" speech. Montgomery, Alabama, March 25, 1965, MLK Online. www.mlkonline.net/ourgod.html.

Dr. King gave one of his most impassioned speeches when he addressed the crowd in front of the Alabama State Capitol on March 25, 1965.

King said the only way southern blacks could achieve equality with whites and have a chance for better lives was by being able to vote. King admitted that the fight for equality would continue to be difficult because so many whites still opposed civil rights for blacks, but King promised African Americans they would eventually prevail if they continued fighting for their rights.

A Violent Ending

When the rally ended, the huge crowd cheerfully dispersed. Thousands of people had come from Selma, and volunteers began driving many of them home. Among the volunteer drivers was Viola Liuzzo, a white mother of five from Detroit who had come to Alabama to support voting rights for blacks. That morning Liuzzo had watched the marchers depart from St. Jude's with Father Tim Deasy, a Catholic priest. Deasy later remembered that Liuzzo had been worried something bad would happen. Deasy said she told him, "I feel it. Somebody is going to get killed."[90]

After dropping some people off at Brown's Chapel, Liuzzo and Leroy Moton, a black teenager helping her drive, headed back to Montgomery to pick up more people. On their way out of Selma, an automobile with four members of the Ku Klux Klan began chasing them. When the car caught up to Liuzzo's vehicle two Klansmen shot her, and her auto crashed off the highway. Liuzzo was killed by two bullets, but Moton survived. The cowardly attack showed southern whites were not yet ready to free blacks from segregation by allowing them to vote.

Chapter Five

Victory! The 1965 Voting Rights Act

On March 21, 1965, Ralph Abernathy was one of the speakers at Brown Chapel African Methodist Episcopal Church before marchers began their historic trek from Selma to Montgomery, Alabama. Abernathy, a veteran of the civil rights movement and a top aide to Martin Luther King Jr., predicted the march would finally give African Americans the right racist whites had so long denied them. Abernathy laughingly told the joyous crowd, "When we get to Montgomery, we are going to go up to Governor Wallace's door and say, 'George, it's all over now. We've got the ballot.'"[91]

The historic march was overwhelmingly successful in showing the nation that blacks in Selma and other southern states were wrongfully being denied the right to vote. The march also influenced many more Americans to support their cause. But the march was not the end of the long, bitter battle blacks had waged to secure the right to vote. Congress still had to pass the Voting Rights Act of 1965, which Lyndon Baines Johnson had proposed six days before marchers proudly and defiantly headed east out of Selma on U.S. 80 for Alabama's state capital.

In the past, senators and representatives from eleven southern states—Alabama, Arkansas, Florida, Georgia, Louisiana,

More than fifty journalists and television reporters from twenty-six states covered the march. Millions of Americans had watched the violence on TV, and it quickly became a national issue.

Mississippi, North Carolina, South Carolina, Tennessee, Texas, and Virginia—had usually succeeded in stopping or weakening legislation to help blacks. Because those southern congressmen knew their states had enough black voters to end segregation, they tried their hardest again to defeat the measure.

This time, however, they failed. One of the main reasons was the powerful effect that television coverage of the events in Selma had on citizens and members of Congress across the nation.

Television Influenced Congress

Until the 1960s many Americans were unaware of or, at the very least, emotionally detached from the struggle southern blacks had been waging for their rights ever since they were freed from slavery at the end of the Civil War. Those attitudes began to change in the 1960s when millions of Americans began watching dramatic news reports of southern blacks fighting for their rights.

From the bus boycott King led in Montgomery in 1955 through the sit-ins, Freedom Rides, and other protests of the 1960s, millions of Americans were horrified by televised scenes of the brutal treatment of blacks by southern state and local officials. Television, a powerful but relatively new medium of mass communication, was a major reason why millions of people living far from Alabama began to care about what was happening in places like Alabama and Mississippi.

Televised reports of Bloody Sunday and other key events in the Selma voting registration drive were among the most dramatic civil rights footage ever aired on television. On March 19 respected *New York Times* political analyst James Reston explained the new power television had to inform the entire nation about an issue of grave social and political importance: "It is the almost instantaneous television reporting of the struggle in the streets of Selma, Ala., that has transformed what would have been mainly a local event a generation ago into a national issue overnight." [92]

The fact that the fight by Selma blacks for the right to vote had become a national concern was evident in how many legislators outside the South began supporting black voting rights. Senator Jacob K. Javits of New York was shocked on February 1 and February 2 when King and hundreds of other people were arrested for peacefully protesting. Javits became one of the first key legislators to say Congress might have to pass legislation to force southern states to allow blacks to register and vote. Congress in the past had been hesitant to directly force states to do such things because of the constitutional concept of states' rights, which said the federal government should allow states to govern themselves as much as possible. But filmed reports of the ugly, sometimes barbaric incidents in Selma led many members of Congress to believe that the need to protect black rights by federal enforcement nullified the sanctity of states' rights.

New York representative Emmanuel Celler was chairman of the House Judiciary Committee, which was holding hearings on the Voting Rights Act. As the marchers made their way from Selma to Montgomery, Celler explained that violence in Selma had forced Congress to act:

> Recent events in Alabama, involving murder, savage brutality, and violence by local police, state troopers, and posses,

have so aroused the nation as to make action by this Congress necessary and speedy. The climate of public opinion throughout the nation has so changed because of the Alabama outrages, as to make assured the passage of this solid bill—a bill that would have been inconceivable a year ago.[93]

The growing furor television coverage generated over Selma voter registration also led fifteen members of the House of Representatives to visit there on February 5 to investigate the situation. On that same day, Jim Clark and his deputies arrested five hundred people. When the delegation returned to Washington that night, representatives Charles Mathis of Maryland and Og-

When New York Republican senator Jacob Javits saw King and hundreds of supporters jailed for peacefully protesting, he became one of the first legislators to say Congress might have to pass legislation to force southern states to allow blacks to register and vote.

den Reid of New York said they believed federal legislation might be needed to help blacks vote. Clark's heavy-handed tactics had once again helped highlight the problem southern blacks faced and created even more sympathy for their plight. Even Joseph Smitherman, who did not support blacks, acknowledged years later that Clark's actions helped blacks gain their rights: "Clark just seemed to get suckered into these situations and make things worse [and] got things stirred up."[94] Clark's dominating presence gave Americans a personification of the racist evil that hurt blacks and made it easier for them to support the fight Selma blacks were waging.

Public officials are influenced by the views of the people who elect them. Congressmen outside the South became concerned with events in Selma because television coverage angered many of their constituents. In a speech on March 10, Wisconsin senator William Proxmire said he knew every senator had received messages from people in their states angry about the brutal treatment of Selma blacks. Proxmire cited a telegram he had received three days after Bloody Sunday from John Lavine, editor of the *Chippewa Herald Telegram* in Chippewa Falls. Even though that small Wisconsin community had few black residents, Lavine said local political leaders and citizens there were outraged at the violence and wanted the federal government to help blacks. "It is not a time for words; it is a time for action,"[95] Lavine wrote Proxmire.

That was the type of reaction, from both lawmakers and citizens, that King had hoped the voter registration drive would create. Because his plan succeeded, it became inevitable that Congress would approve Johnson's bill to help blacks vote.

The Voting Rights Act

On the same day marchers were trudging 16 miles (26km) closer to Montgomery, March 23, a subcommittee of the House Judiciary Committee was holding hearings in Washington, D.C., on the voting rights bill. Earlier legislative attempts to help blacks vote had focused on having federal courts enforce that right, but that tactic had failed because many southern judges were prejudiced against blacks. The new legislative effort would give powers to the attorney general and Department of Justice to force southern counties to register blacks if they had been illegally limiting black voter registration in the past. The bill also provided federal officials with legal methods that allowed them to respond quickly to cases in which state laws or public officials restricted black voting rights.

Southern legislators opposed these powerful new federal enforcement measures because they were key to enabling southern blacks to vote. A main argument opponents used was that the federal government should not have the power to interfere directly in how states registered voters. But on March 18 attorney general Nicholas Katzenbach countered that claim when he testified before the House Judiciary Committee. Katzenbach argued that stronger measures enforced by the federal government were necessary because previous attempts to guarantee blacks the right to register and vote had failed. They had failed because state officials entrusted with carrying them out had allowed the discrimination to continue. Katzenbach said, "The lesson is plain. [Past] statutes have had only minimal effect [on increasing black voting]. They have been too slow."[96] Katzenbach's powerful testimony convinced legislators of the necessity for the new bill.

Opponents also tried to stall passage of the bill by using procedural methods. One Senate technique was the filibuster, in which lawmakers opposing a bill would talk for hours and even days without stopping to prevent a bill's passage. West Virginia senator Robert Byrd in 1964 had spoken for fourteen straight hours in a vain attempt to stop senators from voting on the Civil Rights Act. A former member of the Ku Klux Klan, Byrd said he opposed the bill because he did not think blacks were equal to whites: "Men are not created equal today, and they were not created equal in 1776, when the Declaration of Independence was written. Men and races of men differ in appearance, ways, physical power, mental capacity, creativity and vision."[97]

Those tactics failed in 1964, and they failed again in 1965 against the voting rights bill because so many legislators now supported such measures. In 1965 even opponents of black rights like Byrd realized Congress would pass the bill. While hearings on the voting bill were still under way, Byrd admitted to an aide "You know, you can't stop this bill. We can't deny the Negroes a basic constitutional right to vote."[98] The House passed the bill 328-74 on August 3, and the Senate approved it the next day

President Johnson Signs the Voting Rights Act

President Lyndon Baines Johnson was not known as an eloquent speaker. But on August 6, 1965, when he signed the Voting Rights Act, his televised address to the nation was among his best speeches. The president said:

> Today is a triumph for freedom as huge as any victory that has ever been won on any battlefield. Yet to seize the meaning of this day, we must recall darker times. Three and a half centuries ago the first Negroes arrived at Jamestown [Virginia]. They did not arrive in brave ships in search of a home for freedom. They did not mingle fear and joy, in expectation that in this New World anything would be possible to a man strong enough to reach for it. They came in darkness and they came in chains. And today we strike away the last major shackle of those fierce and ancient bonds. Today the Negro story and the American story fuse and blend. . . . This act flows from a clear and simple wrong. Its only purpose is to right that wrong. Millions of Americans are denied the right to vote because of their color. This law will ensure them the right to vote.

Lyndon Baines Johnson. "Remarks in the Capitol Rotunda at the Signing of the Voting Rights Act, August 6, 1965." *Public Papers of the Presidents of the United States: Lyndon B. Johnson, 1965, 1966.* Washington, DC: Office of the Federal Register, 1965.

With Vice President Hubert Humphrey, civil rights leaders, and congressional leaders from both parties standing behind him, President Johnson signs into law the Voting Rights Act on August 6, 1965.

79-18. On August 6, when Johnson signed the historic measure into law, he was surrounded by civil rights icons like King and Rosa Parks. As a symbolic gesture, Johnson held the signing in the President's Room of the Capitol rotunda where President Abraham Lincoln had signed the Emancipation Proclamation in 1863, freeing the slaves. In a nationally televised speech during the signing ceremony, Johnson said: "The vote is the most powerful instrument ever devised by man for breaking down injustice and destroying the terrible walls which imprison them because they are different from other men. . . . [This] is nothing less than granting every American Negro his freedom to enter the mainstream of American life."[99]

Johnson said the government would waste no time in starting to enforce the new law. He said the Justice Department would immediately send federal examiners to register blacks in fourteen counties that had been slow to register them. The president also said the federal government would file lawsuits to end poll taxes in Texas, Alabama, and Virginia, which had hindered black registration in those states for decades.

The Voting Act Works

Even before Johnson signed the historic bill, black registration had begun to increase in southern states. That was because of efforts the federal government had already made to force those states to register blacks. Also, southern state and local officials realized that Congress was going to pass the voting bill. By the day the president signed the bill, more than nine thousand new black voters had registered in Dallas County. The most dramatic increases were in states that had worked hardest to prevent black voting. In Lowndes County, which bordered Dallas County, there had not been a single black voter just one year earlier. But by the end of the first week of federal intervention in southern states, officials in that county were registering eighty-two blacks a day. In Mississippi, where white violence and intolerance by public officials had severely limited black voting, the number of black voters climbed from 33,000 to 150,000 in just a few months.

Among the new voters were the parents of Sheyann Webb, the eight-year-old Selma girl who had participated in voting protests and narrowly escaped being beaten on the Pettus Bridge on

Bloody Sunday. She explained that her mom and dad did it at her request: "I asked my parents to become registered voters for my birthday present. I thought that my parents could be free citizens if they voted—that's what I wanted for them." Her parents even took Sheyann along with them the first time they voted. "I've never forgotten it,"[100] she said years later.

In its first eighteen months, the act greatly increased the number of black voters in southern states. Federal figures show that at the end of 1966 only four southern states had less than 50 percent of voting-age blacks registered; Mississippi had the lowest rate of 33 percent. But by the November 1968 election even Mississippi's black registration had risen to 59 percent, and black registration overall in the eleven states averaged 62 percent.

African Americans line up to register to vote in Selma. In its first eighteen months after passage, the Voting Rights Act led to a huge increase in the number of registered African American voters.

The Voting Rights Act had forced local officials to register blacks who wanted to vote. But Katzenbach admitted in the spring of 1966 that the huge increase in the number of new black voters was also due to local voter registration drives that helped convince blacks to register and vote. Katzenbach said, "Counties which have seen extensive Negro registration are counties in which registration campaigns have been conducted. In counties without such campaigns even the presence of [federal] examiners has been of limited gain."[101] SCLC, SNCC, and local groups like the Dallas County Voters League were working harder than ever to convince blacks to register now that the new law had made it possible.

By the end of 1966, the number of black voters in the eleven southern states totaled 2,620,359, a figure that rose to 3.1 million two years later. When those new black voters began going to the polls, they began to transform the political systems and lifestyles of southern states.

Black Voters Change the South

It was not very long before the new political strength black voters began to wield in elections helped them have better lives. On May 3, 1966, black votes helped Selma safety director Wilson Baker beat Clark in the election for Dallas County sheriff. The defeat of one of the South's most vicious foes of black rights was an early sign of black voting power. In his book about the Selma demonstrations, Charles E. Fager writes that "[Clark's] political career had been ended, and its ending was the first tangible outgrowth of the blacks' successful struggle to regain the franchise [right to vote]."[102]

Seven years later, black voters elected five of their own to the Selma City Council, including the Reverend Frederick Reese, one of the local leaders of the Selma protests. Even more amazingly, on September 12, 2000, James Perkins Jr., an African American, defeated Smitherman, Selma's longtime mayor, in an election for that office. Perkins's parents had participated in the 1965 protests. But Perkins, who was twelve then, said they would not let him march on Bloody Sunday even though "I cried and cried [to go], but they said no."[103] His election was seen as one of the most important symbols of the political strength southern blacks had

Barack Obama Honors Selma Protesters

Barack Obama, the first African American president, is himself a legacy of the 1965 Selma to Montgomery March. Southern black votes helped elect Obama. In addition, the march led to so many more blacks being elected to public office that the idea of a black president no longer seemed an impossibility. In Selma, Alabama, on March 5, 2007, Obama praised the people who risked their lives to march:

> There were people like Anna Cooper and Marie Foster and Jimmy Lee Jackson and Maurice Olette, C.T. Vivian, Reverend Lowery, John Lewis, who said we can imagine something different and we know there is something out there for us [blacks], too. Thank God, He's made us in His image and we reject the notion that we will for the rest of our lives be confined to a station of inferiority, that we can't aspire to the highest of heights, that our talents can't be expressed to their fullest. And so because of what they endured, because of what they marched, they led a people out of bondage. It's because they marched that we elected councilmen, congress-men. It is because they marched [that] I got the kind of education I got, a law degree, a seat in the Illinois senate and ultimately in the United States senate. It is because they marched that I stand before you here today [as a presidential candidate].

Lynn Sweet. "Obama's Selma Speech, Text as Delivered." *Chicago Sun Times*, March 5, 2007. http://blogs .suntimes.com/sweet/2007/03/obamas_selma_speech_text_as_de.html.

Senator Barack Obama, former president Bill Clinton, and Senator Hillary Clinton commemorate the March to Montgomery at a ceremony in Selma on March 5, 2007.

gained because it happened in Selma, the site of protests that helped blacks gain the right to vote.

Smitherman, who had once opposed black rights, had hung onto the post of mayor for decades after the Selma march by accommodating the needs of black voters. Black voting power also made other white candidates and elected officials court black voters. In 1965 when Clark ran for reelection as sheriff, even he held a barbecue for black voters, but the event was sparsely attended because of his past ugly behavior toward African Americans. This changed attitude toward blacks had first become apparent when the House voted for a second time in 1965 on the Voting Rights Act after the Senate had made some minor changes to the original House version of the bill. In that final vote, some southern representatives who originally opposed it voted for it to curry favor with future black voters.

As the years passed, more and more blacks began to be elected to all levels of state government. This was true not only in the South, where blacks had fought so hard to win the right to vote, but in many other states. The events in Selma had made blacks in other areas of the nation realize how precious the right to vote was, and they began to use it more. The result was that from 1964 to 1970 the number of black elected officials nationwide grew from 300 to 1,469, and by 2007 there were more than 9,500 black elected officials at all levels of government. In Virginia on November 8, 1989, L. Douglas Wilder became the first black elected state governor. In his inaugural address on January 13, 1990, Wilder said his election was proof that the words Thomas Jefferson had written two centuries earlier in the Declaration of Independence were true: "We mark today [the] triumph of an idea. The idea that all men are created equal."[104]

Their new political strength allowed blacks to elect public officials, all the way from county sheriff to governor and U.S. senator, who would honor African American civil rights instead of denying them because of racial prejudice. This new black political strength, however, did not end all the problems African Americans faced in their daily lives. Historian Juan Williams writes:

> Securing the Voting Rights Act was a major victory for the
> Civil Rights Movement. But it was only one part of the larg-

er struggle for dignity, equality, and justice. Segregation lingered in many spheres, black unemployment remained disproportionally high, and violence still flared against black men, women and children. But with the passage of the Voting Rights Act, black citizens had at last gained access to one of the most potent tools of democracy.[105]

Thus even though the Selma protests accomplished what King had desired, they did not end the centuries-long African American struggle for total acceptance and equality with whites. But the

The Greatest Civil Rights Protest

Many historians as well as many of the major figures in the civil rights movement consider the five-day march in 1965 from Selma to Montgomery to be the single most important protest ever for black rights. They believe that the march did more to convince many people in the United States and around the world of the terrible nature of the institutional racism and brutality southern whites had forced southern blacks to endure for so long. This is how historian Fred Powledge sums up the epic march:

> The march from Selma was a majestic moment, television spectacular or not. It was the nation's last great demonstration against the hideousness of overt discrimination—the discrimination of cattle prods and billy sticks and posses; of indignities and systemic fear; the discrimination that said You must stay where you are because we are better than you, and You cannot even vote in our elections. That was the discrimination that the [civil rights] Movement had started out to destroy. As the marchers ticked off the miles between Selma and Montgomery, the Jim Clarks and Bull Connors and George Wallaces grew smaller and less threatening, until at the end they were revealed as the weak, harmless shadows of a once seemingly invincible creature that had roamed the Southland.

Fred Powledge. *Free at Last? The Civil Rights Movement and the People Who Made It*. Boston: Little, Brown, 1991.

dramatic events at Selma had such a powerful effect on bringing blacks closer to this goal that they will always be remembered.

Selma Anniversaries

Selma is considered the culmination of all the protests southern blacks had staged since the first bus boycott in Montgomery a decade earlier. Like the lunch counter sit-ins, bus rides, and countless other marches and demonstrations, it had one goal—to give blacks the same rights their white neighbors had always enjoyed. To honor the Selma protests and keep their memory alive, ceremonies are held annually on the anniversary of Bloody Sunday.

The Reverend Jesse Jackson (center), himself a veteran of "The March," leads a group of marchers across the Edmund Pettus Bridge to commemorate the forty-fifth anniversary of Bloody Sunday on March 7, 2010.

One of the speakers at the March 7, 2010, celebration of the greatest civil rights victory was C.T. Vivian, who was punched in the face by Clark during the protests. "When we think of Selma, this was the high point," Vivian said at Brown Chapel African Methodist Episcopal Church. "This is the place to be once a year." Vivian said Selma was the key event in the black fight for civil rights because it resulted in the Voting Rights Act and because "we knew that the right to vote [for African Americans] would be the right to be human in America."[106]

Notes

Introduction: The Importance of the March

1. Quoted in Alvin Benn. "Activists Complete Final Leg of Selma-to-Montgomery March Re-enactment." *Montgomery Advertiser*, March 14, 2010. www.montgomery advertiser.com/article/20100314/ NEWS01/3140344/Activists+co mplete+final+leg+of+Selma-to-Montgomery+march+re-enactment.

2. Martin Luther King Jr. "Give Us the Ballot." Address delivered at the Prayer Pilgrimage for Freedom, May 17, 1957, Washington, D.C. www.stanford.edu/group/King/ papers/vol4/570517.004-Give_Us_ the_Ballot.html.

3. Quoted in Will Tucker. "Officials, Participants Commemorate 'Bloody Sunday,' Event Marks 45th Anniversary of Selma Bridge Crossing." *University of Alabama Crimson White*, March 8, 2010. www.cw .ua.edu/2010/03/08/officials-participants-commemorate-%E2% 80%98bloody-sunday%E2%80% 99/.

Chapter One: The Modern Civil Rights Movement

4. Quoted in Douglas Brinkley. *Rosa Parks*. New York: Penguin Putnam, 2000, p. 110.

5. Fred Powledge. *Free at Last? The Civil Rights Movement and the People Who Made It*. Boston: Little, Brown, 1991, p. xi.

6. Quoted in Henry Hampton and Steve Fayer. *Voices of Freedom: An Oral History of the Civil Rights Movement from the 1950s Through the 1980s*. New York: Bantam, 1990, p. xxiv.

7. Quoted in Herb Boyd. *We Shall Overcome*. Naperville, IL: Sourcebooks, 2004, pp. 43–44.

8. Quoted in Philip Dray. *At the Hands of Persons Unknown: The Lynching of Black America*. New York: Random House, 2002, p. 111.

9. Quoted in Juan Williams. *Eyes on the Prize: America's Civil Rights Years, 1954–1965*. New York: Viking Penguin, 1987, p. 76.

10. Quoted in Marshall Frady. *Martin Luther King, Jr*. New York: Penguin, 2002, p. 35.

11. Quoted in Jim Bishop. *The Days of Martin Luther King, Jr*. New York: G.P. Putnam's Sons, 1971, p. 41.

12. Quoted in Boyd. *We Shall Overcome*, p. 77.

13. Quoted in Williams. *Eyes on the Prize*, p. 133.

14. Quoted in Boyd. *We Shall Overcome*, p. 85.

15. Quoted in Aldon D. Morris. *The Origins of the Civil Rights Movement: Black Communities Organizing for Change*. New York: Free Press, 1984, p. 232.

16. Quoted in Powledge. *Free at Last*, p. 319.

17. Quoted in Anthony Lewis and *The New York Times. Portrait of a Decade: The Second American Revolution*. New York: Random House, 1964, p. 138.

18. Quoted in Hampton and Fayer. *Voices of Freedom*, p. 142.

19. Quoted in Lewis and *The New York Times. Portrait of a Decade*, p. 141.

20. Quoted in Sanford Wexler. *The Civil Rights Movement: An Eyewitness History*. New York: Facts On File, 1999, p. 212.

Chapter Two: Battle for the Ballot in Selma

21. Quoted in Hampton and Fayer. *Voices of Freedom*, p. 212.

22. Quoted in Boyd. *We Shall Overcome*, p. 190.

23. Quoted in Powledge. *Free at Last*, p. 615.

24. Quoted in Stephen B. Oates. "The Week the World Watched Selma," *American Heritage*, June/July 1982. www.american heritage.com/articles/magazine/ah/1982/4/1982_4_48.shtml.

25. Quoted in John Lewis with Michael D'Orso. *Walking with the Wind: A Memoir of the Movement*. New York: Simon & Schuster, 1998, p. 302.

26. Quoted in John Lewis with D'Orso. *Walking with the Wind*, p. 302.

27. Quoted in Williams. *Eyes on the Prize*, p. 258.

28. Quoted in Lewis with D'Orso. *Walking with the Wind*, p. 303.

29. Quoted in David J. Garrow. *Protest at Selma: Martin Luther King, Jr., and the Voting Rights Act of 1965*. New Haven, CT: Yale University Press, 1978, p. 34.

30. Quoted in Stewart Burns. *To the Mountain Top: Martin Luther King's Sacred Mission to Save America, 1955–1968*. New York: HarperSanFranciso, 2004, p. 262.

31. Martin Luther King Jr. *Where Do We Go from Here: Chaos or Community?* New York: HarperCollins, 1967, p. 51.

32. Quoted in Hampton and Fayer. *Voices of Freedom*, p. 217.

33. Quoted in Williams. *Eyes on the Prize*, p. 254.

34. Quoted in Hampton and Fayer. *Voices of Freedom*, p. 215.

35. Quoted in Charles E. Fager. *Selma 1965: The March That Changed the South*. New York: Charles Scribner's Sons, 1974, p. 9.

36. Lyndon Baines Johnson. "State of the Union Address, 4 January 1965," *American Experience*.

www.pbs.org/wgbh/amex/presidents/
36_l_johnson/psources/ps_union65
.html.

37. Quoted in Fager. *Selma 1965*, p. 29.

38. Quoted in Williams. *Eyes on the Prize*, p. 259.

39. Quoted in Oates. "The Week the World Watched Selma."

40. Quoted in Garrow. *Protest at Selma*, p. 47.

41. Quoted in Williams. *Eyes on the Prize*, p. 260.

Chapter Three: Bloody Sunday and a Symbolic March

42. Quoted in Wexler. *The Civil Rights Movement*, p. 217.

43. Quoted in Garrow. *Protest at Selma*, p. 56.

44. Quoted in Fager. *Selma 1965*, p. 67.

45. Quoted in Williams. *Eyes on the Prize*, p. 265.

46. Quoted in Fager. *Selma 1965*, p. 70.

47. Quoted in Boyd. *We Shall Overcome*, p. 194.

48. Quoted in John Fleming. "The Death of Jimmie Lee Jackson." *Anniston (AL) Star*, March 06, 2005. www.annistonstar.com/pages/full_story/push?article-The+Death+of+Jimmie+Lee+Jackson%20&id=27 46471&instance=special.

49. Quoted in Burns. *To the Mountain Top*, p. 273.

50. Quoted in Hampton and Fayer. *Voices of Freedom*, p. 227.

51. Quoted in Fager. *Selma 1965*, p. 85.

52. Lewis with D'Orso. *Walking with the Wind*, p. 319.

53. Quoted in Williams. *Eyes on the Prize*, p. 268.

54. Quoted in Lori Rozsa. "From the Front Lines of Freedom." *People Weekly*, March 7, 2005, p. 110.

55. Lewis with D'Orso. *Walking with the Wind*, p. 327.

56. Quoted in Rozsa. "From the Front Lines of Freedom," p. 111.

57. Sheyann Webb and Rachel West Nelson. *Selma, Lord, Selma: Childhood Memories of the Civil-Rights Days as Told to Frank Sikora*. Tuscaloosa: University of Alabama Press, 1980, p. 95.

58. Quoted in Oates. "The Week the World Watched Selma."

59. Quoted in Williams. *Eyes on the Prize*, p. 273.

60. Quoted in Robert Dallek. *Flawed Giant: Lyndon Johnson and His Times, 1961–1973*. New York: Oxford University Press, p. 215.

61. Quoted in Williams. *Eyes on the Prize*, p. 273.

62. Quoted in Fager. *Selma 1965*, p. 103.

63. Quoted in Oates. "The Week the World Watched Selma."

64. Quoted in Garrow. *Protest at Selma*, p. 86.

65. Quoted in Williams. *Eyes on the Prize*, p. 268.

66. Quoted in Powledge. *Free at Last?* p. 625.

67. Quoted in Lewis with D'Orso. *Walking with the Wind*, p. 336.

Chapter Four: A Joyous March to Montgomery

68. Quoted in Wexler. *The Civil Rights Movement*, p. 221.

69. Quoted in Hampton and Fayer. *Voices of Freedom*, p. 233.

70. Quoted in Fager. *Selma 1965*, p. 112.

71. Quoted in Dallek. *Flawed Giant*, p. 217.

72. Lyndon Baines Johnson. "We Shall Overcome," speech delivered to a Joint Session of Congress on March 15, 1965. www.americanrhetoric .com/speeches/lbjweshallovercome .html.

73. Quoted in Hampton and Fayer. *Voices of Freedom*, p. 236.

74. Quoted in Webb and Nelson. *Selma, Lord, Selma*, p. 116.

75. Quoted in Lewis with D'Orso. *Walking with the Wind*, p. 325.

76. Quoted in Hampton and Fayer. *Voices of Freedom*, p. 238.

77. Quoted in W.C. Heinz and Bard Lindeman. "The Meaning of the Selma March: Great Day at Tricken Fork," *Saturday Evening Post*, May 22, 1965, p. 32.

78. Quoted in Fager. *Selma 1965*, p. 150.

79. Quoted in Simeon Booker, "50,000 March on Montgomery." *Ebony,* May 1965, p. 78.

80. Quoted in Heinz and Lindeman. "The Meaning of the Selma March," p. 92.

81. Quoted in Booker. "50,000 March on Montgomery," p. 60.

82. Quoted in Elizabeth Levit Spaid. "Selma to Montgomery March Re-enacted by Old Hands, Youth," *Christian Science Monitor*, March 13, 1995, p. 3.

83. Quoted in Lewis with D'Orso. *Walking with the Wind*, p. 343.

84. Quoted in Hampton and Fayer. *Voices of Freedom*, p. 237.

85. Quoted in Heinz and Lindeman. "The Meaning of the Selma March," p. 33.

86. Quoted in Fager. *Selma 1965*, p. 155.

87. Quoted in Civil Rights Movement Veterans Organization. "Selma & the March to Montgomery A Discussion, November–June, 2004–2005," www.crmvet.org/ disc/selma.html.

88. Quoted in Oates. "The Week the World Watched Selma."

89. Martin Luther King Jr. "Our God Is Marching On!" speech, Montgomery, Alabama, March 25, 1965, MLK Online. www.mlkonline.net/ ourgod.html.

90. Quoted in Fager, *Selma 1965*, p. 160.

Chapter Five: Victory! The 1965 Voting Rights Act

91. Quoted in Wexler. *The Civil Rights Movement*, p. 237.

92. James Reston. "Washington: The Rising Spirit of Protest," *New York Times*, March 19, 1965, p. 34.

93. Quoted in Williams. *Eyes on the Prize*, pp. 282–283.

94. Quoted in Webb and Nelson. *Selma, Lord, Selma*, p. 43.

95. Quoted in Garrow. *Protest at Selma*, p. 178.

96. Nicholas Katzenbach. "Voting Rights Act of 1965." *Vital Speeches of the Day*, April 15, 1965, p. 391.

97. Quoted in Eugene Robinson. "Robert Byrd: A Story of Change and Redemption." *Washington Post*, June 29, 2010. www.washingtonpost.com/wp-dyn/content/article/2010/06/28/AR2010062803119.html.

98. Quoted in Williams. *Eyes on the Prize*, p. 285.

99. Lyndon Baines Johnson. "Remarks in the Capitol Rodunda at the Signing of the Voting Rights Act, August 6, 1965." *Public Papers of the Presidents of the United States: Lyndon B. Johnson, 1965, 1966*. Washington, DC: Office of the Federal Register.

100. Quoted in Chuck Stone. "Selma to Montgomery." *National Geographic*, February 2000, p. 98.

101. Quoted in Garrow. *Protest at Selma*, p. 178.

102. Fager. *Selma 1965*, p. 211.

103. Quoted in Florestine Purnell, Lori Rozsam, and Nancy Wilstach. "Bridge Builder." *People Weekly*, November 6, 2000, p. 75.

104. Quoted in *Fort Lauderdale (FL) Sun Sentinel*. "Success Story: Virginia Inaugurates Nation's First Black Elected Governor." January 14, 1990, p. A1.

105. Williams. *Eyes on the Prize*, p. 285.

106. Quoted in *Montgomery Advertiser*. "Selma the 'High Point' in War to Vote, Vivian Says." March 8, 2010. www.montgomeryadvertiser.com/article/20100308/NEWS02/3080310/1009.

Chronology

1929–1941
The United States experiences the Great Depression.

1954
Supreme Court ruling in *Brown v. Board of Education* outlaws segregation in public schools.

1960
On February 1 four black students sit at the whites-only lunch counter at the Woolworth's store in Greensboro, North Carolina.

1961
On May 5 Alan Shepard becomes the first American in space.

1963
The Feminine Mystique by Betty Friedan is published, helping to spark the modern women's rights movement.

November 22: President John F. Kennedy is assassinated; Lyndon Baines Johnson becomes president of the United States.

1964
August 2: U.S. Congress passes the Gulf of Tonkin Resolution granting President Johnson permission to use force in Southeast Asia, marking the beginning of the Vietnam War.

December 10: Martin Luther King Jr. is awarded the Nobel Peace Prize.

1965
January 18–19: Martin Luther King Jr. leads voter registration marches in Selma.

February 1: Civil rights leader Malcom X is assassinated.

February 18: Jimmie Lee Jackson is shot by an Alabama state trooper during a nighttime march in Marion, Alabama; his death six days later triggers the idea for a march from Selma to Montgomery, the Alabama state capital.

March 7: The first march of six hundred people turns into a day known as Bloody Sunday when law enforcement officials attack marchers on the Pettus Bridge so they cannot leave the city.

March 15: President Johnson calls for a Voting Rights Act in a nationally televised speech to Congress.

March 21–25: Protesters march from Selma to Montgomery; they conclude with a rally in Montgomery attended by twenty-five thousand people.

August 6: President Johnson signs the Voting Rights Act of 1965.

1967
Thurgood Marshall is sworn in as the first African American Supreme Court justice.

For More Information

Books

Herbert Aptheker, ed. *A Documentary History of the Negro People in the United States, 1960–1968. Vol. 7: From the Alabama Protests to the Death of Martin Luther King, Jr.* New York: Carol, 1994. This collection of documents, interviews, speeches, and other works provides an interesting look at the civil rights movement in this period.

Herb Boyd, ed. *Autobiography of a People: Three Centuries of African-American History Told by Those Who Lived It.* New York: Doubleday, 2000. Includes firsthand accounts of what it was like for civil rights workers to battle racism.

Clayborne Carson et al., eds. *The Eyes on the Prize Civil Rights Reader: Documents, Speeches, and Firsthand Accounts from the Black Freedom Struggle, 1954–1990.* New York: Viking, 1991. This excellent collection contains information on what happened during the civil rights movement as well as why it happened.

Leon Friedman, ed. *The Civil Rights Reader: Basic Documents of the Civil Rights Movement.* New York: Walker, 1968. This collection of speeches, documents, and other sources provides interesting highlights about civil rights, including personal experiences of many of those involved in the fight.

August Meier, Elliot Rudwick, and John Bracey Jr., eds. *Black Protest in the Sixties: Articles from the "New York Times."* New York: Markus Wiener, 1991. Fine stories from the newspaper's Sunday magazine that delve into the battle for civil rights in this decade.

Howell Raines. *My Soul Is Rested: Movement Days in the Deep South Remembered.* New York: Penguin, 1983. Through interviews with the men and women who lived it, the author provides a fascinating look at what it was like to be a civil rights worker in the sixties.

Michael V. Uschan. *The 1960s: Life on the Front Line in the Fight for Civil Rights.* Detroit: Lucent, 2004. The book traces the fight blacks waged for civil rights in the 1960s.

Websites

The Civil Rights Movement (www.ecsu.ctstateu.edu/depts/edu/textbooks/civilrights). A list of many civil rights websites.

Greensboro Sit-ins: Launch of a Civil Rights Movement (www.sitins.com). Information and pictures on sit-ins by the Greensboro (North Carolina) Public Library and *Greensboro News & Record* newspaper.

MLK Online (www.mlkonline.com). An Internet site dedicated to Martin Luther King Jr.

Places to Visit

National Voting Rights Museum & Institute Selma (www.nvrm .org/). Located at 6 Highway 80 East, Selma, AL 36701, this museum documents the struggle to gain voting rights by southern blacks.

Video

Disney's *Selma, Lord, Selma*, directed by Charles Burnett. Burbank, CA: Walt Disney Home Video, 2004, DVD.

Index

Picture Credits

Cover: James Martin/Birmingham News/ Landov

AP Images, 10, 30, 37, 44, 52, 63, 64, 69, 73, 76, 81, 83

AP Images/Dave Martin, 88

AP Images/Horace Cort, 34, 39

AP Images/str, 23

© Bettmann/Corbis, 32, 41, 46, 49, 51, 59, 78

Carl Iwasaki/Time & Life Pictures/Getty Images, 17

Don Cravens/Time & Life Pictures/Getty Images, 14, 61

Flip Schulke/Corbis, 55

George Tames/New York Times Co./ Getty Images, 19

Hulton Archive/Getty Images, 25

© Jack Moebes/Corbis, 21

Rolls Press/Popperfoto/Getty Images, 68

Roberto Schmidt/AFP/Getty Images, 85

© Steve Schapiro/Corbis, 66

William Lovelace/Express/Getty Images, 70

About the Author

Michael V. Uschan has written over thirty books, including *The Korean War*, for which he won the 2002 Council of Wisconsin Writers Juvenile Nonfiction Award. Mr. Uschan began his career as a writer and editor with United Press International, a wire service that provides stories to newspapers, radio, and television. As journalism is sometimes called "history in a hurry," Mr. Uschan considers writing history books a natural extension of skills he developed in his many years as a working journalist. He and his wife, Barbara, reside in the Milwaukee suburb of Franklin, Wisconsin.